Super Simple

Air Fryer

Cookbook UK 2023

Delicious, Quick & Budget-Friendly Air Fryer Recipes Book for Beginners Incl. Dinners, Sides, Desserts, Snacks, etc. - UK Measurements & Ingredients

Libby Humphries

Warning-Disclaimer

The purpose of this book is to educate and entertain. The author or publisher does not guarantee that anyone following the techniques, suggestions, tips, ideas, or strategies will become successful. The author and publisher shall have neither liability or responsibility to anyone with respect to any loss or damage caused, or alleged to be caused, directly or indirectly by the information contained in this book.

Table of Contents

Chapter 6 Poultry

Chapter 7 Beef, Pork, and Lamb

Chapter 8 Fish and Seafood

Chapter 9 Snacks and Appetizers

Chapter 8 Vegetables and Sides

Chapter 11 Vegetarian Mains

Chapter 12 Desserts

INTRODUCTION

Are you tired of feeling guilty after indulging in your favorite fried foods? Do you want to explore healthier and more convenient ways of cooking without sacrificing flavor? Then join me on a journey of discovering the endless possibilities of air fryer cooking. In this journey, we'll explore a variety of delicious and healthy recipes for different meals and occasions. From crispy fried chicken to juicy burgers, we'll show you how to make your favorite dishes with a fraction of the oil and without losing any of the flavor.

But that's not all - we'll also provide tips and tricks for adapting your favorite traditional recipes to be cooked in an air fryer, so you can enjoy your favorite foods with a healthier twist. And with the convenience of air fryer cooking, you'll be able to whip up meals in a fraction of the time it takes with traditional cooking methods. No more waiting for the oven to preheat or struggling to clean up a greasy mess from frying on the stove.

But don't just take our word for it - join us on this journey and see for yourself how air fryer cooking can revolutionize your kitchen. With each recipe, we'll provide nutritional information, so you can make informed choices about what you're eating. Say goodbye to feeling guilty about indulging in fried foods and hello to a healthier and more convenient way of cooking.

Chapter 1 Air Fryer 101: Understanding the Basics

If you're new to using an air fryer, or considering purchasing one, this book is the ultimate guide to everything air fryer-related! You'll find a wealth of information, tips, and tricks on how to make the most out of your air fryer, as well as a mouthwatering collection of recipes to try. Discover the versatility of your air fryer as we guide you through cooking a variety of meals using a wide range of ingredients. From meats to vegetables, appetizers to desserts, your new kitchen gadget can handle it all - and in the healthiest and cleanest way possible.

But first, let's get to know your air fryer. What exactly is an air fryer and how does it work? This book has got you covered!

What is an Air Fryer?

An air fryer is a cooking appliance that uses hot air instead of oil to cook your food. It is a more advanced and healthier option compared to regular deep fat fryers, which use an abundance of hot oil to cook food, resulting in crispy but extremely unhealthy meals and snacks.

The air fryer uses a convection technique to circulate hot air around the machine, which is powered by a fan that pushes the air deep into the fryer. This ensures that none of the ingredients are missed, and the end result is delicious, crispy food in a fraction of the time. Since the air fryer does not use oil, it avoids the unhealthy saturated fat and artery-clogging effect that deep fat fryers can have.

Using an air fryer results in home-cooked meals that are cost-effective, healthy, and lack the dripping oil that deep fat fryers produce. It is also very easy to use, making it a suitable option for beginners or anyone who wants to save time in the kitchen. Most of the time, you simply place your ingredients into the fryer and let the machine do its job.

In the following chapters, we will explore the versatility and variety of meals and snacks that can be made using an air fryer. This machine is capable of making a wide range of dishes, and we will delve deeper into the wonderful world of the air fryer to provide you with a better understanding of how it works and what it can do for you.

The Advantages of Air Fryer Cooking: Healthy, Easy, and Delicious!

♦ Cook your food quickly and easily: One of the most significant benefits of using an air fryer is that it allows you to cook your food quickly and easily. With the touch of a button, you can have a delicious, crispy meal in no time. This convenience is especially helpful for busy families who may not have the time to prepare elaborate meals every day. Additionally, air fryers are incredibly easy to use, making them an excellent choice for beginners who are just starting to learn their way around the kitchen.

♦ Far healthier than deep fat frying: In addition to being easy to use and convenient, air fryers are far healthier than deep fat frying. Traditional deep frying requires a lot of oil, which can make even healthy foods like vegetables and fish unhealthy. Air fryers, on the other hand, use hot air to cook your food, eliminating the need for excessive amounts of oil. This means that you can enjoy all your favorite fried foods, like chicken wings and french fries, without any of the unhealthy elements of oil.

♦ Versatility in cooking a variety of foods: Another benefit of using an air fryer is its versatility in cooking a variety of foods. From vegetables to meats and even desserts, air fryers can handle it all. They come with various cooking settings and can be used to bake, roast, and grill foods as well. This versatility means that you can use your air fryer to make all sorts of meals, making it an essential appliance in any kitchen.

♦ Make crispy food without harmful oil: One of the best things about using an air fryer is that it gives you crispy food without the unhealthy element of oil. This is particularly helpful if you have children who love crispy fried foods that are terrible for their health. With an air fryer, you can recreate the same effect with far less calories and fat, ensuring that your family is eating healthy without sacrificing taste.

♦ Dishwasher-Safe and easy to clean: Air fryers are also incredibly easy to clean. Most air fryer parts are suitable to be cleaned in the dishwasher, although it's essential to check the instructions of your particular model. Thanks to the lack of added oils or fats, air fryers are much easier to clean than traditional deep fryers, which can be a hassle to clean up after use.

♦ Cooking frozen food with convenience: If you're someone who likes to keep frozen foods in your kitchen, you'll love using an air fryer. Frozen food is cooked to a crisp quickly and easily, saving you time and energy in the kitchen. Alternatively, you can use your air fryer to cook from scratch, ensuring that your meals are always fresh and healthy.

♦ Say goodbye to preheating: Another significant benefit of using an air fryer is that your kitchen won't become overheated when using it, like it would with a deep fat fryer. This makes it a great appliance to use during hot summer months when you don't want to add any extra heat to your home.

♦ Cost-effective cooking method: Finally, air fryers are a cost-effective investment that will allow you to make a huge number of different meals and snacks with ease. While the initial cost may seem steep, the money you'll save on oil and other cooking ingredients will quickly make up for it. Plus, with the ability to make so many different meals, an air fryer is an investment that you'll use for years to come.

In conclusion, air fryers are an excellent investment for anyone looking to eat healthy without sacrificing taste. With their convenience, versatility, and ability to produce crispy foods without added oils or fats, air fryers are a must-have appliance in any kitchen. They're easy to use, easy to clean, and can be used to cook a variety of foods, making them an ideal choice for families on the go. So why not consider adding an air fryer to your kitchen and see for yourself just how useful and beneficial they can be?

Chapter 2 Unlocking the Power of Your Air Fryer: Pro Tips for Perfect Results

Before Purchasing an Air Fryer

When considering buying an air fryer, it's important to keep in mind that there are certain limitations to what can be cooked in it. Any foods with a liquid-style batter should be avoided as they will not cook properly and can make a mess of the machine. However, freezing the batter beforehand and then adding it to the machine can achieve a similar effect. It's also important to note that most air fryers have a limited capacity, so if you plan to cook for a large group of people, you may need to cook in batches.

Aside from the slight limitations, there are some things you need to consider when purchasing your first air fryer:

1.Price

When considering purchasing an air fryer, it's important to keep in mind that the cost can vary depending on the model and features. Generally, larger capacity and more features will come with a higher price tag, while more basic models may be more affordable. It's important to assess your needs and budget before making a purchase.

One way to find an air fryer that fits your budget is to shop around and compare prices from different retailers. Look for sales or promotions that may be available to save some money. It's also worth considering purchasing a refurbished or used air fryer to save money,

although be sure to check the condition and any warranties before buying.

While it may be tempting to go for the most expensive and feature-rich air fryer on the market, it's important to consider whether those features are necessary for your needs. Do you really need a larger capacity if you only plan to use the air fryer for small batches of food? Are advanced features like presets and smart controls worth the extra cost if you just want to fry some chicken wings?

Ultimately, the cost of an air fryer should be balanced against its benefits and how often you plan to use it. If you're someone who enjoys fried foods frequently and wants a healthier alternative to traditional deep frying, investing in a high-quality air fryer may be a worthwhile expense. However, if you only plan to use it occasionally or for small batches of food, a more basic model may be a better fit for your budget.

2.Space

Although the inner capacity of most air fryers is not that much, it's worth noting that these appliances tend to be quite large due to the fan and heating mechanism inside. Therefore, before purchasing an air fryer, it's essential to consider how much space you have available in your kitchen. You should also keep in mind that some models have a bulkier design than others, which may require even more counter or storage space. Additionally, if you plan to use your air fryer frequently, it's a good idea to keep it easily accessible on your kitchen counter to save time and effort when cooking.

3.Features

If you are new to using air fryers, it is important to know that you don't necessarily need a high-end, feature-packed machine. Take the time to explore the different features offered by various models and choose one that suits your needs and comfort level. Keep in mind that some features may be unnecessary and may only increase the cost of the appliance. It's also a good idea to read reviews and compare prices to ensure you're getting the best value for your money. Ultimately, the most important factor is that you feel confident and comfortable using your chosen air fryer.

4.Brand

Choosing a reputable brand can provide peace of mind when investing in an air fryer. Well-known brands often come with a considerable guarantee, which can be essential if you're spending a significant amount of money. However, it's important to note that not all well-known brands may offer the best value for money. Researching and reading reviews from other customers can also help you make an informed decision. Additionally, consider the brand's reputation for customer service and support, in case you encounter any issues with your air fryer.

Maintaining Your Air Fryer

Ensuring proper maintenance of your air fryer is crucial if you want to extend its lifespan. To keep your appliance in good working condition, regular cleaning is essential. Although it might sound like a chore, cleaning an air fryer is relatively easy and straightforward. Ideally, it is best to clean the air fryer after each use. Luckily, most models come with dishwasher-safe parts, making cleaning a breeze. Nonetheless, be sure to consult your user manual to confirm whether your model is dishwasher-safe.

It is vital to avoid using abrasive materials when cleaning the air fryer as the coating inside the appliance is prone to scratches. Therefore, stay away from metallic items, steel wool, and sponges with rough edges. Additionally, it's crucial to avoid submerging the air fryer in water as this can damage the electric components. Keep in mind that the main body of the fryer operates on electricity and needs to be treated with care.

How to Clean Your Air Fryer

Steps to clean your air fryer:
1. Turn off and unplug your air fryer and let it cool down.
2. Remove the basket and the pan.
3. Use a damp cotton cloth to wipe the outside of the main unit.
4. Use warm water and a non-abrasive sponge to wipe the inside of the main unit, being sure to remove any crispy pieces that have stuck to the inner wall.
5. Turn the fryer upside down and wipe the heating section of the appliance.
6. Check the instructions, but most baskets and pans are safe to be placed in the dishwasher. If not, you can wash them with hot water and a soft sponge, making sure to remove any crispy residue.
7. Allow everything to air dry.
8. Reassemble your air fryer.

If you notice an unpleasant smell coming from your air fryer, place half a lemon inside the main basket and pan and let it sit for around 30 minutes. Afterwards, clean as normal and allow to air dry.

Remember to clean your air fryer after every use to keep it in good condition and extend its lifespan. By following these simple steps, you can ensure that your air fryer stays clean and functioning properly.

Air Fryer Troubleshooting

Typically, there are several typical problems that air fryers can encounter. Fortunately, these issues can generally be resolved without requiring any significant repairs or professional help. Let's take a look at some of the most prevalent problems and their solutions.

♦ Food with dry or chewy texture, or even food that turns out to be soggy. It is important to keep in mind that air fryers do not use oil, which can sometimes lead to food being baked instead of fried. If you find that your food is not as crispy as you would like it to be, consider lightly coating it with a small amount of oil to enhance the crispiness. However, it's important to note that high-quality air fryers should not have this issue in the first place. In addition, there are other factors that can affect the crispiness of your food, such as the temperature and cooking time. It's important to follow the instructions carefully and experiment with different cooking times and temperatures to achieve your desired results. Another tip is to avoid overcrowding the air fryer basket, as this can also lead to less crispy results. By following these tips and using a high-quality air fryer, you can ensure that your food is cooked to perfection every time.

♦ White smoke. If you notice white smoke coming from your air fryer, don't panic. It's a common issue and can be easily resolved at home. This occurs when there is a high amount of fat in the food being cooked. While it isn't harmful, it can be frustrating to deal with. To prevent this, it's important to regularly clean the oil collection compartment of the air fryer to ensure that it is not filled with excess fat. You should also avoid overfilling the basket with food, as this can cause the excess fat to overflow and create more smoke. Keeping your air fryer clean and properly maintained is crucial to ensure that it functions efficiently and produces delicious, healthy meals.

♦ No Power. If your air fryer is unresponsive when you turn it on, don't worry too much just yet. There are a few things you can do to troubleshoot the issue before you consider returning it for a replacement or repair. Firstly, check that all the components are correctly connected and that the power cable is securely plugged in. Additionally, make sure that the power switch is turned on and that the timer is set correctly. Some air fryers require you to set the timer before the power kicks in, so this may be the issue. If you've checked all of these things and still no luck, try changing the fuse inside the plug. This is a simple and easy fix that may solve the problem. However, if none of these steps work, it's best to return the air fryer and have it checked or replaced by a professional.

More Tips for Using Air Fryer

We're approaching the next part! But before we dive into that, let's provide you with some last useful tips for when you purchase and start cooking with your brand-new air fryer.

1. Prior to placing your food in the air fryer, heat it up for a few minutes.

2. If your food doesn't have an oily surface, apply a light coating of oil. Meat may not require extra oil, but vegetables and battered foods may benefit from it.

3. To prevent food from sticking, apply a layer of cooking spray to the bottom of the basket.

4. Avoid overcrowding the basket with too much food, as this can hinder proper cooking. It is preferable to cook in smaller batches.

5. When cooking wings or fries, shake them occasionally, every few minutes or so.

6. To achieve optimal crispiness, add a light coating of oil to your food when it is halfway through the cooking process.

7. Using the highest temperature setting is not always the best option for achieving crispness; adjust the temperature according to the type of food being cooked.

A Cookbook for Air Fryer Beginners

When I first purchased my air fryer, I was skeptical about its ability to deliver the same taste and texture as traditional deep frying. However, I was pleasantly surprised by the results. Not only did my air fryer create delicious and crispy fried foods, but it did so with a fraction of the oil, making it a healthier option.

I quickly discovered that my air fryer was not just limited to frying foods. It had the capability to cook an array of dishes from vegetables to desserts. One of my favorite dishes to make in the air fryer is roasted vegetables. The air fryer gives them a crispy texture on the outside while keeping them tender on the inside. I've also made everything from chicken wings to donuts and have been thrilled with the outcome.

In addition to expanding my cooking options, using an air fryer has positively impacted my lifestyle. I no longer have to feel guilty about indulging in fried foods because I know that they are healthier when cooked in the air fryer. The convenience of the air fryer also makes cooking faster and easier, which is a lifesaver for busy weeknights.

The air fryer has transformed the way I cook, and I now find myself reaching for it more often than my oven or stove-top. I've even started experimenting with different techniques and flavors to create unique and delicious dishes. My air fryer has truly opened up a whole new world of cooking possibilities for me.

In conclusion, investing in an air fryer has been one of the best decisions I've made for my cooking and lifestyle. It has not only allowed me to cook delicious and healthier meals but has also made cooking more convenient and efficient. If you're on the fence about getting an air fryer, I highly recommend taking the plunge and experiencing the game-changing benefits for yourself.

What to Expect in this Cookbook?

If you're looking for inspiration for healthy and delicious meals, you've come to the right place. Our air fryer cookbook offers a range of recipes to suit any taste buds, from classic comfort foods to exciting international dishes. We believe that cooking with an air fryer doesn't have to mean sacrificing flavor or texture, and we've designed our recipes to prove just that. Whether you're looking for a quick and easy weeknight dinner or an impressive dish for a special occasion, we've got you covered. Our recipes are also perfect for those who want to meal prep, as air fryers are known for their efficiency and speed in cooking.

In addition to recipes, we'll provide you with helpful tips on how to make the most out of your air fryer, including how to clean and maintain it properly. We also understand that everyone has different dietary needs, which is why we've included options for vegetarians, vegans, and those who follow a gluten-free diet.

With our air fryer cookbook, you'll be able to enjoy all your favorite foods in a healthier and more convenient way. So get ready to discover a whole new world of cooking possibilities with us.

Chapter 3 Breakfasts

Chapter 3 Breakfasts

Simple Scotch Eggs

Prep time: 5 minutes | Cook time: 25 minutes | Serves 4

4 large hard boiled eggs	8 slices thick-cut bacon
1 (340 g) package pork sausage meat	4 wooden toothpicks, soaked in water for at least 30 minutes

1. Slice the sausage meat into four parts and place each part into a large circle. 2. Put an egg into each circle and wrap it in the sausage. Put in the refrigerator for 1 hour. 3. Preheat the air fryer to 234ºC. 4. Make a cross with two pieces of thick-cut bacon. Put a wrapped egg in the center, fold the bacon over top of the egg, and secure with a toothpick. 5. Air fry in the preheated air fryer for 25 minutes. 6. Serve immediately.

Breakfast Sausage and Cauliflower

Prep time: 5 minutes | Cook time: 45 minutes | Serves 4

450 g sausage meat, cooked and crumbled	plus more for topping
475 ml double/whipping cream	8 eggs, beaten
1 head cauliflower, chopped	Salt and ground black pepper, to taste
235 ml grated Cheddar cheese,	

1. Preheat the air fryer to 176ºC. 2. In a large bowl, mix the sausage, cream, chopped cauliflower, cheese and eggs. Sprinkle with salt and ground black pepper. 3. Pour the mixture into a greased casserole dish. Bake in the preheated air fryer for 45 minutes or until firm. 4. Top with more Cheddar cheese and serve.

Green Eggs and Ham

Prep time: 5 minutes | Cook time: 10 minutes | Serves 2

1 large Hass avocado, halved and pitted	½ teaspoon fine sea salt
2 thin slices ham	¼ teaspoon ground black pepper
2 large eggs	60 ml shredded Cheddar cheese (omit for dairy-free)
2 tablespoons chopped spring onions, plus more for garnish	

1. Preheat the air fryer to 204ºC. 2. Place a slice of ham into the cavity of each avocado half. Crack an egg on top of the ham, then sprinkle on the green onions, salt, and pepper. 3. Place the avocado halves in the air fryer cut side up and air fry for 10 minutes, or until the egg is cooked to your desired doneness. Top with the cheese (if using) and air fry for 30 seconds more, or until the cheese is melted. Garnish with chopped green onions. 4. Best served fresh. Store extras in an airtight container in the fridge for up to 4 days. Reheat in a preheated 176ºC air fryer for a few minutes, until warmed through.

Sausage and Egg Breakfast Burrito

Prep time: 5 minutes | Cook time: 30 minutes | Serves 6

6 eggs	(removed from casings)
Salt and pepper, to taste	120 ml salsa
Cooking oil	6 medium (8-inch) flour tortillas
120 ml chopped red pepper	120 ml shredded Cheddar cheese
120 ml chopped green pepper	
230 g chicken sausage meat	

1. In a medium bowl, whisk the eggs. Add salt and pepper to taste. 2. Place a skillet on medium-high heat. Spray with cooking oil. Add the eggs. Scramble for 2 to 3 minutes, until the eggs are fluffy. Remove the eggs from the skillet and set aside. 3. If needed, spray the skillet with more oil. Add the chopped red and green bell peppers. Cook for 2 to 3 minutes, until the peppers are soft. 4. Add the sausage meat to the skillet. Break the sausage into smaller pieces using a spatula or spoon. Cook for 3 to 4 minutes, until the sausage is brown. 5. Add the salsa and scrambled eggs. Stir to combine. Remove the skillet from heat. 6. Spoon the mixture evenly onto the tortillas. 7. To form the burritos, fold the sides of each tortilla in toward the middle and then roll up from the bottom. You can secure each burrito with a toothpick. Or you can moisten the outside edge of the tortilla with a small amount of water. I prefer to use a cooking brush, but you can also dab with your fingers. 8. Spray the burritos with cooking oil and place them in the air fryer. Do not stack. Cook the burritos in batches if they do not all fit in the basket. Air fry at 204ºC for 8 minutes. 9. Open the air fryer and flip the burritos. Cook for an additional 2 minutes or until crisp. 10. If necessary, repeat steps 8 and 9 for the remaining burritos. 11. Sprinkle the Cheddar cheese over the burritos. Cool before serving.

Gluten-Free Granola Cereal

Prep time: 7 minutes | Cook time: 30 minutes |
Makes 820 ml

Oil, for spraying
350 ml gluten-free rolled oats
120 ml chopped walnuts
120 ml chopped almonds
120 ml pumpkin seeds
60 ml maple syrup or honey

1 tablespoon toasted sesame oil
or vegetable oil
1 teaspoon ground cinnamon
½ teaspoon salt
120 ml dried cranberries

1. Preheat the air fryer to 120ºC. Line the air fryer basket with parchment and spray lightly with oil. (Do not skip the step of lining the basket; the parchment will keep the granola from falling through the holes.) 2. In a large bowl, mix together the oats, walnuts, almonds, pumpkin seeds, maple syrup, sesame oil, cinnamon, and salt. 3. Spread the mixture in an even layer in the prepared basket. 4. Cook for 30 minutes, stirring every 10 minutes. 5. Transfer the granola to a bowl, add the dried cranberries, and toss to combine. 6. Let cool to room temperature before storing in an airtight container.

Everything Bagels

Prep time: 15 minutes | Cook time: 14 minutes |
Makes 6 bagels

415 ml shredded Mozzarella
cheese or goat cheese
Mozzarella
2 tablespoons unsalted butter or
coconut oil
1 large egg, beaten
1 tablespoon apple cider

vinegar
235 ml blanched almond flour
1 tablespoon baking powder
⅛ teaspoon fine sea salt
1½ teaspoons sesame seeds or
za'atar

1. Make the dough: Put the Mozzarella and butter in a large microwave-safe bowl and microwave for 1 to 2 minutes, until the cheese is entirely melted. Stir well. Add the egg and vinegar. Using a hand mixer on medium, combine well. Add the almond flour, baking powder, and salt and, using the mixer, combine well. 2. Lay a piece of parchment paper on the countertop and place the dough on it. Knead it for about 3 minutes. The dough should be a little sticky but pliable. (If the dough is too sticky, chill it in the refrigerator for an hour or overnight.) 3. Preheat the air fryer to 176ºC. Spray a baking sheet or pie pan that will fit into your air fryer with avocado oil. 4. Divide the dough into 6 equal portions. Roll 1 portion into a log that is 6 inches long and about ½ inch thick. Form the log into a circle and seal the edges together, making a bagel shape. Repeat with the remaining portions of dough, making 6 bagels. 5. Place the bagels on the greased baking sheet. Spray the bagels with avocado oil and top with everything bagel seasoning, pressing the seasoning into the dough with your hands. 6. Place the bagels in the air fryer and bake for 14 minutes, or

until cooked through and golden brown, flipping after 6 minutes. 7. Remove the bagels from the air fryer and allow them to cool slightly before slicing them in half and serving. Store leftovers in an airtight container in the fridge for up to 4 days or in the freezer for up to a month.

Turkey Sausage Breakfast Pizza

Prep time: 15 minutes | Cook time: 24 minutes | Serves 2

4 large eggs, divided
1 tablespoon water
½ teaspoon garlic powder
½ teaspoon onion granules
½ teaspoon dried oregano
2 tablespoons coconut flour
3 tablespoons grated Parmesan
cheese

120 ml shredded low-moisture
Mozzarella or other melting
cheese
1 link cooked turkey sausage,
chopped (about 60 g)
2 sun-dried tomatoes, finely
chopped
2 sping onions, thinly sliced

1. Preheat the air fryer to 204ºC. Line a cake pan with parchment paper and lightly coat the paper with olive oil. 2. In a large bowl, whisk 2 of the eggs with the water, garlic powder, onion granules, and dried oregano. Add the coconut flour, breaking up any lumps with your hands as you add it to the bowl. Stir the coconut flour into the egg mixture, mixing until smooth. Stir in the Parmesan cheese. Allow the mixture to rest for a few minutes until thick and dough-like. 3. Transfer the mixture to the prepared pan. Use a spatula to spread it evenly and slightly up the sides of the pan. Air fry until the crust is set but still light in color, about 10 minutes. Top with the cheeses, sausage, and sun-dried tomatoes. 4. Break the remaining 2 eggs into a small bowl, then slide them onto the pizza. Return the pizza to the air fryer. Air fry 10 to 14 minutes until the egg whites are set and the yolks are the desired doneness. Top with the scallions and allow to rest for 5 minutes before serving.

Pizza Eggs

Prep time: 5 minutes | Cook time: 10 minutes | Serves 2

235 ml shredded Mozzarella
cheese
7 slices pepperoni, chopped
1 large egg, whisked

¼ teaspoon dried oregano
¼ teaspoon dried parsley
¼ teaspoon garlic powder
¼ teaspoon salt

1. Place Mozzarella in a single layer on the bottom of an ungreased round nonstick baking dish. Scatter pepperoni over cheese, then pour egg evenly around baking dish. 2. Sprinkle with remaining ingredients and place into air fryer basket. Adjust the temperature to 166ºC and bake for 10 minutes. When cheese is brown and egg is set, dish will be done. 3. Let cool in dish 5 minutes before serving.

Bacon and Spinach Egg Muffins

Prep time: 7 minutes | Cook time: 12 to 14 minutes | Serves 6

6 large eggs	(optional)
60 ml double (whipping) cream	180 ml frozen chopped spinach,
½ teaspoon sea salt	thawed and drained
¼ teaspoon freshly ground	4 strips cooked bacon, crumbled
black pepper	60 g shredded Cheddar cheese
¼ teaspoon cayenne pepper	

1. In a large bowl (with a spout if you have one), whisk together the eggs, double cream, salt, black pepper, and cayenne pepper (if using). 2. Divide the spinach and bacon among 6 silicone muffin cups. Place the muffin cups in your air fryer basket. 3. Divide the egg mixture among the muffin cups. Top with the cheese. 4. Set the air fryer to 150°C. Bake for 12 to 14 minutes, until the eggs are set and cooked through.

Cajun Breakfast Sausage

Prep time: 10 minutes | Cook time: 15 to 20 minutes | Serves 8

680 g 85% lean turkey mince	1 teaspoon Cajun seasoning
3 cloves garlic, finely chopped	1 teaspoon dried thyme
¼ onion, grated	½ teaspoon paprika
1 teaspoon Tabasco sauce	½ teaspoon cayenne

1. Preheat the air fryer to 188°C. 2. In a large bowl, combine the turkey, garlic, onion, Tabasco, Cajun seasoning, thyme, paprika, and cayenne. Mix with clean hands until thoroughly combined. Shape into 16 patties, about ½ inch thick. (Wet your hands slightly if you find the sausage too sticky to handle.) 3. Working in batches if necessary, arrange the patties in a single layer in the air fryer basket. Pausing halfway through the cooking time to flip the patties, air fry for 15 to 20 minutes until a thermometer inserted into the thickest portion registers 74°C.

Maple Granola

Prep time: 5 minutes | Cook time: 40 minutes | Makes 475 ml

235 ml rolled oats	sunflower
3 tablespoons pure maple syrup	¼ teaspoon sea salt
1 tablespoon sugar	¼ teaspoon ground cinnamon
1 tablespoon neutral-flavored	¼ teaspoon vanilla extract
oil, such as refined coconut or	

1. Insert the crisper plate into the basket and the basket into the unit. Preheat the unit by selecting BAKE, setting the temperature to 120°C, and setting the time to 3 minutes. Select START/STOP to begin. 2. In a medium bowl, stir together the oats, maple syrup, sugar, oil, salt, cinnamon, and vanilla until thoroughly combined. Transfer the granola to a 6-by-2-inch round baking pan. 3. Once the unit is preheated, place the pan into the basket. 4. Select BAKE, set the temperature to 120°C and set the time to 40 minutes. Select START/STOP to begin. 5. After 10 minutes, stir the granola well. Resume cooking, stirring the granola every 10 minutes, for a total of 40 minutes, or until the granola is lightly browned and mostly dry. 6. When the cooking is complete, place the granola on a plate to cool. It will become crisp as it cools. Store the completely cooled granola in an airtight container in a cool, dry place for 1 to 2 weeks.

Gold Avocado

Prep time: 5 minutes | Cook time: 6 minutes | Serves 4

2 large avocados, sliced	120 ml flour
¼ teaspoon paprika	2 eggs, beaten
Salt and ground black pepper,	235 ml bread crumbs
to taste	

1. Preheat the air fryer to 204°C. 2. Sprinkle paprika, salt and pepper on the slices of avocado. 3. Lightly coat the avocados with flour. Dredge them in the eggs, before covering with bread crumbs. 4. Transfer to the air fryer and air fry for 6 minutes. 5. Serve warm.

Honey-Apricot Granola with Greek Yoghurt

Prep time: 10 minutes | Cook time: 30 minutes | Serves 6

235 ml rolled oats	1 teaspoon ground cinnamon
60 ml dried apricots, diced	¼ teaspoon ground nutmeg
60 ml almond slivers	¼ teaspoon salt
60 ml walnuts, chopped	2 tablespoons sugar-free dark
60 ml pumpkin seeds	chocolate chips (optional)
60 to 80 ml honey, plus more	700 ml fat-free plain Greek
for drizzling	yoghurt
1 tablespoon olive oil	

1. Preheat the air fryer to 128°C. Line the air fryer basket with parchment paper. 2. In a large bowl, combine the oats, apricots, almonds, walnuts, pumpkin seeds, honey, olive oil, cinnamon, nutmeg, and salt, mixing so that the honey, oil, and spices are well distributed. 3. Pour the mixture onto the parchment paper and spread it into an even layer. 4. Bake for 10 minutes, then shake or stir and spread back out into an even layer. Continue baking for 10 minutes more, then repeat the process of shaking or stirring the mixture. Bake for an additional 10 minutes before removing from the air fryer. 5. Allow the granola to cool completely before stirring in the chocolate chips (if using) and pouring into an airtight container for storage. 6. For each serving, top 120 ml Greek yoghurt with 80 ml granola and a drizzle of honey, if needed.

Gyro Breakfast Patties with Tzatziki

Prep time: 10 minutes | Cook time: 20 minutes per batch | Makes 16

patties

Patties:

900 g lamb or beef mince	½ teaspoon fine sea salt
120 ml diced red onions	½ teaspoon garlic powder, or 1
60 ml sliced black olives	clove garlic, minced
2 tablespoons tomato sauce	¼ teaspoon dried dill, or 1
1 teaspoon dried oregano leaves	teaspoon finely chopped fresh
2 cloves garlic, minced	dill
1 teaspoon fine sea salt	For Garnish/Serving:
Tzatziki:	120 ml crumbled feta cheese
235 ml full-fat sour cream	(about 60 g)
1 small cucumber, chopped	Diced red onions
	Sliced black olives
	Sliced cucumbers

1. Preheat the air fryer to 176ºC. 2. Place the lamb, onions, olives, tomato sauce, oregano, garlic, and salt in a large bowl. Mix well to combine the ingredients. 3. Using your hands, form the mixture into sixteen 3-inch patties. Place about 5 of the patties in the air fryer and air fry for 20 minutes, flipping halfway through. Remove the patties and place them on a serving platter. Repeat with the remaining patties. 4. While the patties cook, make the tzatziki: Place all the ingredients in a small bowl and stir well. Cover and store in the fridge until ready to serve. Garnish with ground black pepper before serving. 5. Serve the patties with a dollop of tzatziki, a sprinkle of crumbled feta cheese, diced red onions, sliced black olives, and sliced cucumbers. 6. Store leftovers in an airtight container in the refrigerator for up to 5 days or in the freezer for up to a month. Reheat the patties in a preheated 200ºC air fryer for a few minutes, until warmed through.

Apple Rolls

Prep time: 20 minutes | Cook time: 20 to 24 minutes | Makes 12 rolls

Apple Rolls:

475 ml plain flour, plus more	sugar
for dusting	1 teaspoon ground cinnamon
2 tablespoons granulated sugar	1 large Granny Smith apple,
1 teaspoon salt	peeled and diced
3 tablespoons butter, at room	1 to 2 tablespoons oil
temperature	Icing:
180 ml milk, whole or semi-	120 ml icing sugar
skimmed	½ teaspoon vanilla extract
120 ml packed light brown	2 to 3 tablespoons milk, whole
	or semi-skimmed

Make the Apple Rolls 1. In a large bowl, whisk the flour, granulated sugar, and salt until blended. Stir in the butter and milk briefly until a sticky dough forms. 2. In a small bowl, stir together the brown sugar, cinnamon, and apple. 3. Place a piece of parchment paper on a work surface and dust it with flour. Roll the dough on the prepared surface to ¼ inch thickness. 4. Spread the apple mixture over the dough. Roll up the dough jelly roll-style, pinching the ends to seal. Cut the dough into 12 rolls. 5. Preheat the air fryer to 160ºC. 6. Line the air fryer basket with parchment paper and spritz it with oil. Place 6 rolls on the prepared parchment. 7. Bake for 5 minutes. Flip the rolls and bake for 5 to 7 minutes more until lightly browned. Repeat with the remaining rolls. Make the Icing 8. In a medium bowl, whisk the icing sugar, vanilla, and milk until blended. 9. Drizzle over the warm rolls.

Veggie Frittata

Prep time: 7 minutes | Cook time: 21 to 23 minutes | Serves 2

Avocado oil spray	85 g shredded sharp Cheddar
60 ml diced red onion	cheese, divided
60 ml diced red pepper	½ teaspoon dried thyme
60 ml finely chopped broccoli	Sea salt and freshly ground
4 large eggs	black pepper, to taste

1. Spray a pan well with oil. Put the onion, pepper, and broccoli in the pan, place the pan in the air fryer, and set to 176ºC. Bake for 5 minutes. 2. While the vegetables cook, beat the eggs in a medium bowl. Stir in half of the cheese, and season with the thyme, salt, and pepper. 3. Add the eggs to the pan and top with the remaining cheese. Set the air fryer to 176ºC. Bake for 16 to 18 minutes, until cooked through.

Easy Buttermilk Biscuits

Prep time: 5 minutes | Cook time: 18 minutes | Makes 16 biscuits

600 ml plain flour	½ teaspoon baking soda
1 tablespoon baking powder	8 tablespoons (1 stick) unsalted
1 teaspoon coarse or flaky salt	butter, at room temperature
1 teaspoon sugar	235 ml buttermilk, chilled

1. Stir together the flour, baking powder, salt, sugar, and baking powder in a large bowl. 2. Add the butter and stir to mix well. Pour in the buttermilk and stir with a rubber spatula just until incorporated. 3. Place the dough onto a lightly floured surface and roll the dough out to a disk, ½ inch thick. Cut out the biscuits with a 2-inch round cutter and re-roll any scraps until you have 16 biscuits. 4. Preheat the air fryer to 164ºC. 5. Working in batches, arrange the biscuits in the air fryer basket in a single layer. Bake for about 18 minutes until the biscuits are golden brown. 6. Remove from the basket to a plate and repeat with the remaining biscuits. 7. Serve hot.

Simple Cinnamon Toasts

Prep time: 5 minutes | Cook time: 4 minutes | Serves 4

1 tablespoon salted butter
2 teaspoons ground cinnamon
4 tablespoons sugar
½ teaspoon vanilla extract
10 bread slices

1. Preheat the air fryer to 192°C. 2. In a bowl, combine the butter, cinnamon, sugar, and vanilla extract. Spread onto the slices of bread. 3. Put the bread inside the air fryer and bake for 4 minutes or until golden brown. 4. Serve warm.

Broccoli-Mushroom Frittata

Prep time: 10 minutes | Cook time: 20 minutes | Serves 2

1 tablespoon olive oil
350 ml broccoli florets, finely chopped
120 ml sliced brown mushrooms
60 ml finely chopped onion
½ teaspoon salt
¼ teaspoon freshly ground black pepper
6 eggs
60 ml Parmesan cheese

1. In a nonstick cake pan, combine the olive oil, broccoli, mushrooms, onion, salt, and pepper. Stir until the vegetables are thoroughly coated with oil. Place the cake pan in the air fryer basket and set the air fryer to 204°C. Air fry for 5 minutes until the vegetables soften. 2. Meanwhile, in a medium bowl, whisk the eggs and Parmesan until thoroughly combined. Pour the egg mixture into the pan and shake gently to distribute the vegetables. Air fry for another 15 minutes until the eggs are set. 3. Remove from the air fryer and let sit for 5 minutes to cool slightly. Use a silicone spatula to gently lift the frittata onto a plate before serving.

Jalapeño and Bacon Breakfast Pizza

Prep time: 5 minutes | Cook time: 10 minutes | Serves 2

235 ml shredded Mozzarella cheese
30 g cream cheese, broken into small pieces
4 slices cooked bacon, chopped
60 ml chopped pickled jalapeños
1 large egg, whisked
¼ teaspoon salt

1. Place Mozzarella in a single layer on the bottom of an ungreased round nonstick baking dish. Scatter cream cheese pieces, bacon, and jalapeños over Mozzarella, then pour egg evenly around baking dish. 2. Sprinkle with salt and place into air fryer basket. Adjust the temperature to 166°C and bake for 10 minutes. When cheese is brown and egg is set, pizza will be done. 3. Let cool on a large plate 5 minutes before serving.

Homemade Cherry Breakfast Tarts

Prep time: 15 minutes | Cook time: 20 minutes | Serves 6

Tarts:
2 refrigerated piecrusts
80 ml cherry preserves
1 teaspoon cornflour
Cooking oil

Frosting:
120 ml vanilla yoghurt
30 g cream cheese
1 teaspoon stevia
Rainbow sprinkles

Make the Tarts 1. Place the piecrusts on a flat surface. Using a knife or pizza cutter, cut each piecrust into 3 rectangles, for 6 total. (I discard the unused dough left from slicing the edges.) 2. In a small bowl, combine the preserves and cornflour. Mix well. 3. Scoop 1 tablespoon of the preserves mixture onto the top half of each piece of piecrust. 4. Fold the bottom of each piece up to close the tart. Using the back of a fork, press along the edges of each tart to seal. 5. Spray the breakfast tarts with cooking oil and place them in the air fryer. I do not recommend stacking the breakfast tarts. They will stick together if stacked. You may need to prepare them in two batches. Bake at 375°F for 10 minutes. 6. Allow the breakfast tarts to cool fully before removing from the air fryer. 7. If necessary, repeat steps 5 and 6 for the remaining breakfast tarts. Make the Frosting 8. In a small bowl, combine the yoghurt, cream cheese, and stevia. Mix well. 9. Spread the breakfast tarts with frosting and top with sprinkles, and serve.

Bacon, Egg, and Cheese Roll Ups

Prep time: 15 minutes | Cook time: 15 minutes | Serves 4

2 tablespoons unsalted butter
60 ml chopped onion
½ medium green pepper, seeded and chopped
6 large eggs
12 slices bacon
235 ml shredded sharp Cheddar cheese
120 ml mild salsa, for dipping

1. In a medium skillet over medium heat, melt butter. Add onion and pepper to the skillet and sauté until fragrant and onions are translucent, about 3 minutes. 2. Whisk eggs in a small bowl and pour into skillet. Scramble eggs with onions and peppers until fluffy and fully cooked, about 5 minutes. Remove from heat and set aside. 3. On work surface, place three slices of bacon side by side, overlapping about ¼ inch. Place 60 ml scrambled eggs in a heap on the side closest to you and sprinkle 60 ml cheese on top of the eggs. 4. Tightly roll the bacon around the eggs and secure the seam with a toothpick if necessary. Place each roll into the air fryer basket. 5. Adjust the temperature to 176°C and air fry for 15 minutes. Rotate the rolls halfway through the cooking time. 6. Bacon will be brown and crispy when completely cooked. Serve immediately with salsa for dipping.

Turkey Breakfast Sausage Patties

Prep time: 5 minutes | Cook time: 10 minutes | Serves 4

1 tablespoon chopped fresh thyme	½ teaspoon onion granules
1 tablespoon chopped fresh sage	½ teaspoon garlic powder
1¼ teaspoons coarse or flaky salt	⅛ teaspoon crushed red pepper flakes
1 teaspoon chopped fennel seeds	⅛ teaspoon freshly ground black pepper
¾ teaspoon smoked paprika	450 g lean turkey mince
	120 ml finely minced sweet apple (peeled)

1. Thoroughly combine the thyme, sage, salt, fennel seeds, paprika, onion granules, garlic powder, red pepper flakes, and black pepper in a medium bowl. 2. Add the turkey mince and apple and stir until well incorporated. Divide the mixture into 8 equal portions and shape into patties with your hands, each about ¼ inch thick and 3 inches in diameter. 3. Preheat the air fryer to 204ºC. 4. Place the patties in the air fryer basket in a single layer. You may need to work in batches to avoid overcrowding. 5. Air fry for 5 minutes. Flip the patties and air fry for 5 minutes, or until the patties are nicely browned and cooked through. 6. Remove from the basket to a plate and repeat with the remaining patties. 7. Serve warm.

Hearty Cheddar Biscuits

Prep time: 10 minutes | Cook time: 22 minutes |
Makes 8 biscuits

550 ml self-raising flour	plus more to melt on top
2 tablespoons sugar	315 ml buttermilk
120 ml butter, frozen for 15 minutes	235 ml plain flour, for shaping
120 ml grated Cheddar cheese,	1 tablespoon butter, melted

1. Line a buttered 7-inch metal cake pan with parchment paper or a silicone liner. 2. Combine the flour and sugar in a large mixing bowl. Grate the butter into the flour. Add the grated cheese and stir to coat the cheese and butter with flour. Then add the buttermilk and stir just until you can no longer see streaks of flour. The dough should be quite wet. 3. Spread the plain (not self-raising) flour out on a small cookie sheet. With a spoon, scoop 8 evenly sized balls of dough into the flour, making sure they don't touch each other. With floured hands, coat each dough ball with flour and toss them gently from hand to hand to shake off any excess flour. Put each floured dough ball into the prepared pan, right up next to the other. This will help the biscuits rise, rather than spreading out. 4. Preheat the air fryer to 192ºC. 5. Transfer the cake pan to the basket of the air fryer. Let the ends of the aluminum foil sling hang across the cake pan before returning the basket to the air fryer. 6. Air fry for 20 minutes. Check the biscuits twice to make sure they are not getting too brown on top. If they are, re-arrange the aluminum foil strips to cover any brown parts. After 20 minutes, check the biscuits by inserting a toothpick into the center of the biscuits. It should come out clean. If it needs a little more time, continue to air fry for two extra minutes. Brush the tops of the biscuits with some melted butter and sprinkle a little more grated cheese on top if desired. Pop the basket back into the air fryer for another 2 minutes. 7. Remove the cake pan from the air fryer. Let the biscuits cool for just a minute or two and then turn them out onto a plate and pull apart. Serve immediately.

Mexican Breakfast Pepper Rings

Prep time: 5 minutes | Cook time: 10 minutes | Serves 4

Olive oil	4 eggs
1 large red, yellow, or orange pepper, cut into four ¾-inch rings	Salt and freshly ground black pepper, to taste
	2 teaspoons salsa

1. Preheat the air fryer to 176ºC. Lightly spray a baking pan with olive oil. 2. Place 2 bell pepper rings on the pan. Crack one egg into each bell pepper ring. Season with salt and black pepper. 3. Spoon ½ teaspoon of salsa on top of each egg. 4. Place the pan in the air fryer basket. Air fry until the yolk is slightly runny, 5 to 6 minutes or until the yolk is fully cooked, 8 to 10 minutes. 5. Repeat with the remaining 2 pepper rings. Serve hot.

Chimichanga Breakfast Burrito

Prep time: 10 minutes | Cook time: 10 minutes | Serves 2

2 large (10- to 12-inch) flour tortillas	4 corn tortilla chips, crushed
120 ml canned refried beans (pinto or black work equally well)	120 ml grated chili cheese
	12 pickled jalapeño slices
	1 tablespoon vegetable oil
4 large eggs, cooked scrambled	Guacamole, salsa, and sour cream, for serving (optional)

1. Place the tortillas on a work surface and divide the refried beans between them, spreading them in a rough rectangle in the center of the tortillas. Top the beans with the scrambled eggs, crushed chips, cheese, and jalapeños. Fold one side over the fillings, then fold in each short side and roll up the rest of the way like a burrito. 2. Brush the outside of the burritos with the oil, then transfer to the air fryer, seam-side down. Air fry at 176ºC until the tortillas are browned and crisp and the filling is warm throughout, about 10 minutes. 3. Transfer the chimichangas to plates and serve warm with guacamole, salsa, and sour cream, if you like.

Denver Omelette

Prep time: 5 minutes | Cook time: 8 minutes | Serves 1

2 large eggs
60 ml unsweetened, unflavoured almond milk
¼ teaspoon fine sea salt
⅛ teaspoon ground black pepper
60 ml diced ham (omit for vegetarian)
60 ml diced green and red

peppers
2 tablespoons diced spring onions, plus more for garnish
60 ml shredded Cheddar cheese (about 30 g) (omit for dairy-free)
Quartered cherry tomatoes, for serving (optional)

1. Preheat the air fryer to 176°C. Grease a cake pan and set aside. 2. In a small bowl, use a fork to whisk together the eggs, almond milk, salt, and pepper. Add the ham, peppers, and spring onions. Pour the mixture into the greased pan. Add the cheese on top (if using). 3. Place the pan in the basket of the air fryer. Bake for 8 minutes, or until the eggs are cooked to your liking. 4. Loosen the omelette from the sides of the pan with a spatula and place it on a serving plate. Garnish with spring onions and serve with cherry tomatoes, if desired. Best served fresh.

Mushroom-and-Tomato Stuffed Hash Browns

Prep time: 10 minutes | Cook time: 20 minutes | Serves 4

Olive oil cooking spray
1 tablespoon plus 2 teaspoons olive oil, divided
110 g baby mushrooms, diced
1 spring onion, white parts and green parts, diced

1 garlic clove, minced
475 ml shredded potatoes
½ teaspoon salt
¼ teaspoon black pepper
1 plum tomato, diced
120 ml shredded mozzarella

1. Preheat the air fryer to 192°C. Lightly coat the inside of a 6-inch cake pan with olive oil cooking spray. 2. In a small skillet, heat 2 teaspoons olive oil over medium heat. Add the mushrooms, spring onion, and garlic, and cook for 4 to 5 minutes, or until they have softened and are beginning to show some color. Remove from heat. 3. Meanwhile, in a large bowl, combine the potatoes, salt, pepper, and the remaining tablespoon olive oil. Toss until all potatoes are well coated. 4. Pour half of the potatoes into the bottom of the cake pan. Top with the mushroom mixture, tomato, and mozzarella. Spread the remaining potatoes over the top. 5. Bake in the air fryer for 12 to 15 minutes, or until the top is golden brown. 6. Remove from the air fryer and allow to cool for 5 minutes before slicing and serving.

Southwestern Ham Egg Cups

Prep time: 5 minutes | Cook time: 12 minutes | Serves 2

4 (30 g) slices wafer-thin ham
4 large eggs
2 tablespoons full-fat sour cream
60 ml diced green pepper

2 tablespoons diced red pepper
2 tablespoons diced brown onion
120 ml shredded medium Cheddar cheese

1. Place one slice of ham on the bottom of four baking cups. 2. In a large bowl, whisk eggs with sour cream. Stir in green pepper, red pepper, and onion. 3. Pour the egg mixture into ham-lined baking cups. Top with Cheddar. Place cups into the air fryer basket. 4. Adjust the temperature to 160°C and bake for 12 minutes or until the tops are browned. 5. Serve warm.

Potatoes Lyonnaise

Prep time: 10 minutes | Cook time: 31 minutes | Serves 4

1 sweet/mild onion, sliced
1 teaspoon butter, melted
1 teaspoon brown sugar
2 large white potatoes (about 450 g in total), sliced ½-inch

thick
1 tablespoon vegetable oil
Salt and freshly ground black pepper, to taste

1. Preheat the air fryer to 188°C. 2. Toss the sliced onions, melted butter and brown sugar together in the air fryer basket. Air fry for 8 minutes, shaking the basket occasionally to help the onions cook evenly. 3. While the onions are cooking, bring a saucepan of salted water to a boil on the stovetop. Par-cook the potatoes in boiling water for 3 minutes. Drain the potatoes and pat them dry with a clean kitchen towel. 4. Add the potatoes to the onions in the air fryer basket and drizzle with vegetable oil. Toss to coat the potatoes with the oil and season with salt and freshly ground black pepper. 5. Increase the air fryer temperature to 204°C and air fry for 20 minutes, tossing the vegetables a few times during the cooking time to help the potatoes brown evenly. 6. Season with salt and freshly ground black pepper and serve warm.

Chapter 4 Family Favorites

Chapter 4 Family Favorites

Beignets

Prep time: 30 minutes | Cook time: 6 minutes |
Makes 9 beignets

Oil, for greasing and spraying
700 ml plain flour, plus more for dusting
1½ teaspoons salt
1 (2¼-teaspoon) active dry yeast

235 ml milk
2 tablespoons packed light brown sugar
1 tablespoon unsalted butter
1 large egg
235 ml icing sugar

Oil a large bowl. In a small bowl, mix together the flour, salt, and yeast. Set aside. Pour the milk into a glass measuring cup and microwave in 1-minute intervals until it boils. In a large bowl, mix together the brown sugar and butter. Pour in the hot milk and whisk until the sugar has dissolved. Let cool to room temperature. Whisk the egg into the cooled milk mixture and fold in the flour mixture until a dough forms. On a lightly floured work surface, knead the dough for 3 to 5 minutes. Place the dough in the oiled bowl and cover with a clean kitchen towel. Let rise in a warm place for about 1 hour, or until doubled in size. Roll the dough out on a lightly floured work surface until it's about ¼ inch thick. Cut the dough into 3-inch squares and place them on a lightly floured baking sheet. Cover loosely with a kitchen towel and let rise again until doubled in size, about 30 minutes. Line the air fryer basket with parchment and spray lightly with oil. Place the dough squares in the prepared basket and spray lightly with oil. You may need to work in batches, depending on the size of your air fryer. Air fry at 200ºC for 3 minutes, flip, spray with oil, and cook for another 3 minutes, until crispy. Dust with the icing sugar before serving.

Steak and Vegetable Kebabs

Prep time: 15 minutes | Cook time: 5 to 7 minutes |
Serves 4

2 tablespoons balsamic vinegar
2 teaspoons olive oil
½ teaspoon dried marjoram
⅛ teaspoon freshly ground black pepper

340 g silverside steak, cut into 1-inch pieces
1 red pepper, sliced
16 button mushrooms
235 ml cherry tomatoes

In a medium bowl, stir together the balsamic vinegar, olive oil, marjoram, and black pepper. Add the steak and stir to coat. Let stand for 10 minutes at room temperature. Alternating items, thread the beef, red pepper, mushrooms, and tomatoes onto 8 bamboo or metal skewers that fit in the air fryer. Air fry at 200ºC for 5 to 7 minutes, or until the beef is browned and reaches at least 64ºC on a meat thermometer. Serve immediately.

Cheesy Roasted Sweet Potatoes

Prep time: 7 minutes | Cook time: 18 to 23 minutes |
Serves 4

2 large sweet potatoes, peeled and sliced
1 teaspoon olive oil
1 tablespoon white balsamic

vinegar
1 teaspoon dried thyme
60 ml grated Parmesan cheese

In a large bowl, drizzle the sweet potato slices with the olive oil and toss. Sprinkle with the balsamic vinegar and thyme and toss again. Sprinkle the potatoes with the Parmesan cheese and toss to coat. Roast the slices, in batches, in the air fryer basket at 204ºC for 18 to 23 minutes, tossing the sweet potato slices in the basket once during cooking, until tender. Repeat with the remaining sweet potato slices. Serve immediately.

Veggie Tuna Melts

Prep time: 15 minutes | Cook time: 7 to 11 minutes |
Serves 4

2 low-salt wholemeal English muffins, split
1 (170 g) can chunk light low-salt tuna, drained
235 ml shredded carrot
80 ml chopped mushrooms
2 spring onions, white and

green parts, sliced
80 ml fat-free Greek yoghurt
2 tablespoons low-salt wholegrain mustard
2 slices low-salt low-fat Swiss cheese, halved

Place the English muffin halves in the air fryer basket. Air fry at 172ºC for 3 to 4 minutes, or until crisp. Remove from the basket and set aside. In a medium bowl, thoroughly mix the tuna, carrot, mushrooms, spring onions, yoghurt, and mustard. Top each half of the muffins with one-fourth of the tuna mixture and a half slice of Swiss cheese. Air fry for 4 to 7 minutes, or until the tuna mixture is hot and the cheese melts and starts to brown. Serve immediately.

Bacon-Wrapped Hot Dogs

Prep time: 5 minutes | Cook time: 10 minutes | Serves 4

Oil, for spraying	4 hot dog buns
4 bacon slices	Toppings of choice
4 beef hot dogs	

Line the air fryer basket with parchment and spray lightly with oil. Wrap a strip of bacon tightly around each hot dog, taking care to cover the tips so they don't get too crispy. Secure with a toothpick at each end to keep the bacon from shrinking. Place the hot dogs in the prepared basket. Air fry at 192°C for 8 to 9 minutes, depending on how crispy you like the bacon. For extra-crispy, cook the hot dogs at 204°C for 6 to 8 minutes. Place the hot dogs in the buns, return them to the air fryer, and cook for another 1 to 2 minutes, or until the buns are warm. Add your desired toppings and serve.

Pork Stuffing Meatballs

Prep time: 10 minutes | Cook time: 12 minutes | Makes 35 meatballs

Oil, for spraying	1 tablespoon dried thyme
680 g minced pork	1 teaspoon salt
235 ml breadcrumbs	1 teaspoon freshly ground black
120 ml milk	pepper
60 ml minced onion	1 teaspoon finely chopped fresh
1 large egg	parsley
1 tablespoon dried rosemary	

Line the air fryer basket with parchment and spray lightly with oil. In a large bowl, mix together the minced pork, breadcrumbs, milk, onion, egg, rosemary, thyme, salt, black pepper, and parsley. Roll about 2 tablespoons of the mixture into a ball. Repeat with the rest of the mixture. You should have 30 to 35 meatballs. Place the meatballs in the prepared basket in a single layer, leaving space between each one. You may need to work in batches, depending on the size of your air fryer. Air fry at 200°C for 10 to 12 minutes, flipping after 5 minutes, or until golden brown and the internal temperature reaches 72°C.

Meatball Subs

Prep time: 15 minutes | Cook time: 19 minutes | Serves 6

Oil, for spraying	1 tablespoon minced garlic
450 g 15% fat minced beef	1 large egg
120 ml Italian breadcrumbs (mixed breadcrumbs, Italian seasoning and salt)	1 teaspoon salt
	1 teaspoon freshly ground black pepper
1 tablespoon dried minced onion	6 sub rolls
	1 (510 g) jar marinara sauce
350 ml shredded Mozzarella cheese	

Oil, for spraying 450 g 15% fat minced beef 120 ml Italian breadcrumbs (mixed breadcrumbs, Italian seasoning and salt) 1 tablespoon dried minced onion 1 tablespoon minced garlic 1 large egg 1 teaspoon salt 1 teaspoon freshly ground black pepper 6 sub rolls 1 (510 g) jar marinara sauce 350 ml shredded Mozzarella cheese

Fried Green Tomatoes

Prep time: 15 minutes | Cook time: 6 to 8 minutes | Serves 4

4 medium green tomatoes	120 ml panko breadcrumbs
80 ml plain flour	2 teaspoons olive oil
2 egg whites	1 teaspoon paprika
60 ml almond milk	1 clove garlic, minced
235 ml ground almonds	

Rinse the tomatoes and pat dry. Cut the tomatoes into ½-inch slices, discarding the thinner ends. Put the flour on a plate. In a shallow bowl, beat the egg whites with the almond milk until frothy. And on another plate, combine the almonds, breadcrumbs, olive oil, paprika, and garlic and mix well. Dip the tomato slices into the flour, then into the egg white mixture, then into the almond mixture to coat. Place four of the coated tomato slices in the air fryer basket. Air fry at 204°C for 6 to 8 minutes or until the tomato coating is crisp and golden brown. Repeat with remaining tomato slices and serve immediately.

Fish and Vegetable Tacos

Prep time: 15 minutes | Cook time: 9 to 12 minutes | Serves 4

450 g white fish fillets, such as sole or cod	1 large carrot, grated
	120 ml low-salt salsa
2 teaspoons olive oil	80 ml low-fat Greek yoghurt
3 tablespoons freshly squeezed lemon juice, divided	4 soft low-salt wholemeal tortillas
350 ml chopped red cabbage	

Brush the fish with the olive oil and sprinkle with 1 tablespoon of lemon juice. Air fry in the air fryer basket at 200°C for 9 to 12 minutes, or until the fish just flakes when tested with a fork. Meanwhile, in a medium bowl, stir together the remaining 2 tablespoons of lemon juice, the red cabbage, carrot, salsa, and yoghurt. When the fish is cooked, remove it from the air fryer basket and break it up into large pieces. Offer the fish, tortillas, and the cabbage mixture, and let each person assemble a taco.

Beef Jerky

Prep time: 30 minutes | Cook time: 2 hours | Serves 8

Oil, for spraying

450 g silverside steak, cut into thin, short slices

60 ml soy sauce

3 tablespoons packed light brown sugar

1 tablespoon minced garlic

1 teaspoon ground ginger

1 tablespoon water

Line the air fryer basket with parchment and spray lightly with oil. Place the steak, soy sauce, brown sugar, garlic, ginger, and water in a zip-top plastic bag, seal, and shake well until evenly coated. Refrigerate for 30 minutes. Place the steak in the prepared basket in a single layer. You may need to work in batches, depending on the size of your air fryer. Air fry at 82ºC for at least 2 hours. Add more time if you like your jerky a bit tougher.

Chapter 5 Fast and Easy Everyday Favourites

Chapter 5 Fast and Easy Everyday Favourites

Baked Cheese Sandwich

Prep time: 5 minutes | Cook time: 8 minutes | Serves 2

2 tablespoons mayonnaise	8 slices hot capicola or
4 thick slices sourdough bread	prosciutto
4 thick slices Brie cheese	

Preheat the air fryer to 176°C. Spread the mayonnaise on one side of each slice of bread. Place 2 slices of bread in the air fryer basket, mayonnaise-side down. Place the slices of Brie and capicola on the bread and cover with the remaining two slices of bread, mayonnaise-side up. Bake for 8 minutes, or until the cheese has melted. Serve immediately.

Cheesy Chilli Toast

Prep time: 5 minutes | Cook time: 5 minutes | Serves 1

2 tablespoons grated Parmesan cheese	room temperature
	10 to 15 thin slices serrano
2 tablespoons grated Mozzarella cheese	chilli or jalapeño
	2 slices sourdough bread
2 teaspoons salted butter, at	½ teaspoon black pepper

Preheat the air fryer to 164°C. In a small bowl, stir together the Parmesan, Mozzarella, butter, and chillies. Spread half the mixture onto one side of each slice of bread. Sprinkle with the pepper. Place the slices, cheese-side up, in the air fryer basket. Bake for 5 minutes, or until the cheese has melted and started to brown slightly. Serve immediately.

Scalloped Veggie Mix

Prep time: 10 minutes | Cook time: 15 minutes | Serves 4

1 Yukon Gold or other small white potato, thinly sliced	60 ml minced onion
	3 garlic cloves, minced
1 small sweet potato, peeled and thinly sliced	180 ml 2 percent milk
	2 tablespoons cornflour
1 medium carrot, thinly sliced	½ teaspoon dried thyme

Preheat the air fryer to 192°C. In a baking pan, layer the potato,

sweet potato, carrot, onion, and garlic. In a small bowl, whisk the milk, cornflour, and thyme until blended. Pour the milk mixture evenly over the vegetables in the pan. Bake for 15 minutes. Check the casserole—it should be golden brown on top, and the vegetables should be tender. Serve immediately.

Beetroot Salad with Lemon Vinaigrette

Prep time: 10 minutes | Cook time: 12 to 15 minutes | Serves 4

6 medium red and golden beetroots, peeled and sliced	Cooking spray
	Vinaigrette:
1 teaspoon olive oil	2 teaspoons olive oil
¼ teaspoon rock salt	2 tablespoons chopped fresh
120 ml crumbled feta cheese	chives
2 L mixed greens	Juice of 1 lemon

Preheat the air fryer to 182°C. In a large bowl, toss the beetroots, olive oil, and rock salt. Spray the air fryer basket with cooking spray, then place the beetroots in the basket and air fry for 12 to 15 minutes or until tender. While the beetroots cook, make the vinaigrette in a large bowl by whisking together the olive oil, lemon juice, and chives. Remove the beetroots from the air fryer, toss in the vinaigrette, and allow to cool for 5 minutes. Add the feta and serve on top of the mixed greens.

Easy Devils on Horseback

Prep time: 5 minutes | Cook time: 7 minutes | Serves 12

24 small pitted prunes (128 g)	8 slices centre-cut bacon, cut
60 ml crumbled blue cheese, divided	crosswise into thirds

Preheat the air fryer to 204°C. Halve the prunes lengthwise, but don't cut them all the way through. Place ½ teaspoon of cheese in the centre of each prune. Wrap a piece of bacon around each prune and secure the bacon with a toothpick. Working in batches, arrange a single layer of the prunes in the air fryer basket. Air fry for about 7 minutes, flipping halfway, until the bacon is cooked through and crisp. Let cool slightly and serve warm.

Herb-Roasted Veggies

Prep time: 10 minutes | Cook time: 14 to 18 minutes | Serves 4

1 red pepper, sliced	80 ml diced red onion
1 (230 g) package sliced mushrooms	3 garlic cloves, sliced
235 ml green beans, cut into 2-inch pieces	1 teaspoon olive oil
	½ teaspoon dried basil
	½ teaspoon dried tarragon

Preheat the air fryer to 176°C. In a medium bowl, mix the red pepper, mushrooms, green beans, red onion, and garlic. Drizzle with the olive oil. Toss to coat. Add the herbs and toss again. Place the vegetables in the air fryer basket. Roast for 14 to 18 minutes, or until tender. Serve immediately.

Air Fried Shishito Peppers

Prep time: 5 minutes | Cook time: 5 minutes | Serves 4

230 g shishito or Padron peppers (about 24)	Coarse sea salt, to taste
1 tablespoon olive oil	Lemon wedges, for serving
	Cooking spray

Preheat the air fryer to 204°C. Spritz the air fryer basket with cooking spray. Toss the peppers with olive oil in a large bowl to coat well. Arrange the peppers in the preheated air fryer. Air fryer for 5 minutes or until blistered and lightly charred. Shake the basket and sprinkle the peppers with salt halfway through the cooking time. Transfer the peppers onto a plate and squeeze the lemon wedges on top before serving.

Air Fried Courgette Sticks

Prep time: 5 minutes | Cook time: 20 minutes | Serves 4

1 medium courgette, cut into 48 sticks	1 tablespoon melted margarine
60 ml seasoned breadcrumbs	Cooking spray

Preheat the air fryer to 182°C. Spritz the air fryer basket with cooking spray and set aside. In 2 different shallow bowls, add the seasoned breadcrumbs and the margarine. One by one, dredge the courgette sticks into the margarine, then roll in the breadcrumbs to coat evenly. Arrange the crusted sticks on a plate. Place the courgette sticks in the prepared air fryer basket. Work in two batches to avoid overcrowding. Air fry for 10 minutes, or until golden brown and crispy. Shake the basket halfway through to cook evenly. When the cooking time is over, transfer the fries to a wire rack. Rest for 5 minutes and serve warm.

Crunchy Fried Okra

Prep time: 5 minutes | Cook time: 8 to 10 minutes | Serves 4

235 ml self-raising yellow cornmeal (alternatively add 1 tablespoon baking powder to cornmeal)	1 teaspoon salt
1 teaspoon Italian-style seasoning	½ teaspoon freshly ground black pepper
1 teaspoon paprika	2 large eggs, beaten
	475 ml okra slices
	Cooking spray

Preheat the air fryer to 204°C. Line the air fryer basket with parchment paper. In a shallow bowl, whisk the cornmeal, Italian-style seasoning, paprika, salt, and pepper until blended. Place the beaten eggs in a second shallow bowl. Add the okra to the beaten egg and stir to coat. Add the egg and okra mixture to the cornmeal mixture and stir until coated. Place the okra on the parchment and spritz it with oil. Air fry for 4 minutes. Shake the basket, spritz the okra with oil, and air fry for 4 to 6 minutes more until lightly browned and crispy. Serve immediately.

Easy Roasted Asparagus

Prep time: 5 minutes | Cook time: 6 minutes | Serves 4

450 g asparagus, trimmed and halved crosswise	Salt and pepper, to taste
1 teaspoon extra-virgin olive oil	Lemon wedges, for serving

Preheat the air fryer to 204°C. Toss the asparagus with the oil, ⅛ teaspoon salt, and ⅛ teaspoon pepper in bowl. Transfer to air fryer basket. Place the basket in air fryer and roast for 6 to 8 minutes, or until tender and bright green, tossing halfway through cooking. Season with salt and pepper and serve with lemon wedges.

Air Fried Tortilla Chips

Prep time: 5 minutes | Cook time: 10 minutes | Serves 4

4 six-inch corn tortillas, cut in half and slice into thirds	¼ teaspoon rock salt
1 tablespoon rapeseed oil	Cooking spray

Preheat the air fryer to 182°C. Spritz the air fryer basket with cooking spray. On a clean work surface, brush the tortilla chips with rapeseed oil, then transfer the chips in the preheated air fryer. Air fry for 10 minutes or until crunchy and lightly browned. Shake the basket and sprinkle with salt halfway through the cooking time. Transfer the chips onto a plate lined with paper towels. Serve immediately.

Peppery Brown Rice Fritters

Prep time: 10 minutes | Cook time: 8 to 10 minutes | Serves 4

1 (284 g) bag frozen cooked brown rice, thawed

1 egg

3 tablespoons brown rice flour

80 ml finely grated carrots

80 ml minced red pepper

2 tablespoons minced fresh basil

3 tablespoons grated Parmesan cheese

2 teaspoons olive oil

Preheat the air fryer to 192ºC. In a small bowl, combine the thawed rice, egg, and flour and mix to blend. Stir in the carrots, pepper, basil, and Parmesan cheese. Form the mixture into 8 fritters and drizzle with the olive oil. Put the fritters carefully into the air fryer basket. Air fry for 8 to 10 minutes, or until the fritters are golden brown and cooked through. Serve immediately.

Sweet Corn and Carrot Fritters

Prep time: 10 minutes | Cook time: 8 to 11 minutes | Serves 4

Prep time: 10 minutes | Cook time: 8 to 11 minutes | Serves 4

Preheat the air fryer to 176ºC. Place the grated carrot in a colander and press down to squeeze out any excess moisture. Dry it with a paper towel. Combine the carrots with the remaining ingredients. Mould 1 tablespoon of the mixture into a ball and press it down with your hand or a spoon to flatten it. Repeat until the rest of the mixture is used up. Spritz the balls with cooking spray. Arrange in the air fryer basket, taking care not to overlap any balls. Bake for 8 to 11 minutes, or until they're firm. Serve warm.

Cheesy Potato Patties

Prep time: 5 minutes | Cook time: 10 minutes | Serves 8

900 g white potatoes

120 ml finely chopped spring onions

½ teaspoon freshly ground black pepper, or more to taste

1 tablespoon fine sea salt

½ teaspoon hot paprika

475 ml shredded Colby or Monterey Jack cheese

60 ml rapeseed oil

235 ml crushed crackers

Preheat the air fryer to 182ºC. Boil the potatoes until soft. Dry them off and peel them before mashing thoroughly, leaving no lumps. Combine the mashed potatoes with spring onions, pepper, salt, paprika, and cheese. Mould the mixture into balls with your hands and press with your palm to flatten them into patties. In a shallow dish, combine the rapeseed oil and crushed crackers. Coat the patties in the crumb mixture. Bake the patties for about 10 minutes, in multiple batches if necessary. Serve hot.

Air Fried Broccoli

Prep time: 5 minutes | Cook time: 6 minutes | Serves 1

4 egg yolks

60 ml butter, melted

475 ml coconut flour

Salt and pepper, to taste

475 ml broccoli florets

Preheat the air fryer to 204ºC. In a bowl, whisk the egg yolks and melted butter together. Throw in the coconut flour, salt and pepper, then stir again to combine well. Dip each broccoli floret into the mixture and place in the air fryer basket. Air fry for 6 minutes in batches if necessary. Take care when removing them from the air fryer and serve immediately.

Chapter 6 Poultry

Chapter 6 Poultry

Chipotle Drumsticks

Prep time: 15 minutes | Cook time: 20 minutes | Serves 4

1 tablespoon tomato paste
½ teaspoon chipotle powder
¼ teaspoon apple cider vinegar
¼ teaspoon garlic powder

8 chicken drumsticks
½ teaspoon salt
⅛ teaspoon ground black pepper

1. In a small bowl, combine tomato paste, chipotle powder, vinegar, and garlic powder. 2. Sprinkle drumsticks with salt and pepper, then place into a large bowl and pour in tomato paste mixture. Toss or stir to evenly coat all drumsticks in mixture. 3. Place drumsticks into ungreased air fryer basket. Adjust the temperature to 200°C and air fry for 25 minutes, turning drumsticks halfway through cooking. Drumsticks will be dark red with an internal temperature of at least 76°C when done. Serve warm.

Spicy Chicken Thighs and Gold Potatoes

Prep time: 5 minutes | Cook time: 25 minutes | Serves 4

4 bone-in, skin-on chicken thighs
½ teaspoon kosher salt or ¼ teaspoon fine salt
2 tablespoons melted unsalted butter
2 teaspoons Worcestershire sauce
2 teaspoons curry powder
1 teaspoon dried oregano leaves

½ teaspoon dry mustard
½ teaspoon granulated garlic
¼ teaspoon paprika
¼ teaspoon hot pepper sauce
Cooking oil spray
4 medium Yukon gold potatoes, chopped
1 tablespoon extra-virgin olive oil

1. Sprinkle the chicken thighs on both sides with salt. 2. In a medium bowl, stir together the melted butter, Worcestershire sauce, curry powder, oregano, dry mustard, granulated garlic, paprika, and hot pepper sauce. Add the thighs to the sauce and stir to coat. 3. Insert the crisper plate into the basket and the basket into the unit. Preheat the unit by selecting AIR FRY, setting the temperature to 200°C, and setting the time to 3 minutes. Select START/STOP to begin. 4. Once the unit is preheated, spray the crisper plate with cooking oil. In the basket, combine the potatoes and olive oil and toss to coat. 5. Add the wire rack to the air fryer and place the chicken thighs on top. 6. Select AIR FRY, set the temperature to 200°C, and set the time to 25 minutes. Select START/STOP to begin. 7. After 19 minutes check the chicken thighs. If a food

thermometer inserted into the chicken registers 76°C, transfer them to a clean plate, and cover with aluminum foil to keep warm. If they aren't cooked to 76°C, resume cooking for another 1 to 2 minutes until they are done. Remove them from the unit along with the rack. 8. Remove the basket and shake it to distribute the potatoes. Reinsert the basket to resume cooking for 3 to 6 minutes, or until the potatoes are crisp and golden brown. 9. When the cooking is complete, serve the chicken with the potatoes.

Spinach and Feta Stuffed Chicken Breasts

Prep time: 10 minutes | Cook time: 27 minutes | Serves 4

1 (280 g) package frozen spinach, thawed and drained well
80 g feta cheese, crumbled
½ teaspoon freshly ground

black pepper
4 boneless chicken breasts
Salt and freshly ground black pepper, to taste
1 tablespoon olive oil

1. Prepare the filling. Squeeze out as much liquid as possible from the thawed spinach. Rough chop the spinach and transfer it to a mixing bowl with the feta cheese and the freshly ground black pepper. 2. Prepare the chicken breast. Place the chicken breast on a cutting board and press down on the chicken breast with one hand to keep it stabilized. Make an incision about 1-inch long in the fattest side of the breast. Move the knife up and down inside the chicken breast, without poking through either the top or the bottom, or the other side of the breast. The inside pocket should be about 3-inches long, but the opening should only be about 1-inch wide. If this is too difficult, you can make the incision longer, but you will have to be more careful when cooking the chicken breast since this will expose more of the stuffing. 3. Once you have prepared the chicken breasts, use your fingers to stuff the filling into each pocket, spreading the mixture down as far as you can. 4. Preheat the air fryer to 190°C. 5. Lightly brush or spray the air fryer basket and the chicken breasts with olive oil. Transfer two of the stuffed chicken breasts to the air fryer. Air fry for 12 minutes, turning the chicken breasts over halfway through the cooking time. Remove the chicken to a resting plate and air fry the second two breasts for 12 minutes. Return the first batch of chicken to the air fryer with the second batch and air fry for 3 more minutes. When the chicken is cooked, an instant read thermometer should register 76°C in the thickest part of the chicken, as well as in the stuffing. 6. Remove the chicken breasts and let them rest on a cutting board for 2 to 3 minutes. Slice the chicken on the bias and serve with the slices fanned out.

Garlic Soy Chicken Thighs

Prep time: 10 minutes | Cook time: 30 minutes | Serves 1 to 2

2 tablespoons chicken stock

2 tablespoons reduced-sodium soy sauce

1½ tablespoons sugar

4 garlic cloves, smashed and peeled

2 large spring onions, cut into 2- to 3-inch batons, plus more, thinly sliced, for garnish

2 bone-in, skin-on chicken thighs (198 to 225 g each)

1. Preheat the air fryer to 190°C. 2. In a metal cake pan, combine the chicken stock, soy sauce, and sugar and stir until the sugar dissolves. Add the garlic cloves, spring onions, and chicken thighs, turning the thighs to coat them in the marinade, then resting them skin-side up. Place the pan in the air fryer and bake, flipping the thighs every 5 minutes after the first 10 minutes, until the chicken is cooked through and the marinade is reduced to a sticky glaze over the chicken, about 30 minutes. 3. Remove the pan from the air fryer and serve the chicken thighs warm, with any remaining glaze spooned over top and sprinkled with more sliced spring onions.

Israeli Chicken Schnitzel

Prep time: 5 minutes | Cook time: 10 minutes | Serves 4

2 large boneless, skinless chicken breasts, each weighing about 450 g

125 g all-purpose flour

2 teaspoons garlic powder

2 teaspoons kosher salt

1 teaspoon black pepper

1 teaspoon paprika

2 eggs beaten with 2 tablespoons water

250 g panko bread crumbs

Vegetable oil spray

Lemon juice, for serving

1. Preheat the air fryer to 190°C. 2. Place 1 chicken breast between 2 pieces of plastic wrap. Use a mallet or a rolling pin to pound the chicken until it is ¼ inch thick. Set aside. Repeat with the second breast. Whisk together the flour, garlic powder, salt, pepper, and paprika on a large plate. Place the panko in a separate shallow bowl or pie plate. 3. Dredge 1 chicken breast in the flour, shaking off any excess, then dip it in the egg mixture. Dredge the chicken breast in the panko, making sure to coat it completely. Shake off any excess panko. Place the battered chicken breast on a plate. Repeat with the second chicken breast. 4. Spray the air fryer basket with oil spray. Place 1 of the battered chicken breasts in the basket and spray the top with oil spray. Air fry until the top is browned, about 5 minutes. Flip the chicken and spray the second side with oil spray. Air fry until the second side is browned and crispy and the internal temperature reaches 76°C. Remove the first chicken breast from the air fryer and repeat with the second chicken breast. 5. Serve hot with lemon juice.

Sweet and Spicy Turkey Meatballs

Prep time: 15 minutes | Cook time: 15 minutes | Serves 6

Olive oil

450 g lean turkey mince

60 g whole-wheat panko bread crumbs

1 egg, beaten

1 tablespoon soy sauce

60 ml plus 1 tablespoon hoisin

sauce, divided

2 teaspoons minced garlic

⅛ teaspoon salt

⅛ teaspoon freshly ground black pepper

1 teaspoon Sriracha

1. Spray the air fryer basket lightly with olive oil. 2. In a large bowl, mix together the turkey, panko bread crumbs, egg, soy sauce, 1 tablespoon of hoisin sauce, garlic, salt, and black pepper. 3. Using a tablespoon, form 24 meatballs. 4. In a small bowl, combine the remaining 60 ml of hoisin sauce and Sriracha to make a glaze and set aside. 5. Place the meatballs in the air fryer basket in a single layer. You may need to cook them in batches. 6. Air fry at 180°C for 8 minutes. Brush the meatballs generously with the glaze and cook until cooked through, an additional 4 to 7 minutes.

Gochujang Chicken Wings

Prep time: 15 minutes | Cook time: 25 minutes | Serves 4

Wings:

900 g chicken wings

1 teaspoon kosher salt

1 teaspoon black pepper or gochugaru (Korean red pepper)

Sauce:

2 tablespoons gochujang (Korean chili paste)

1 tablespoon mayonnaise

1 tablespoon toasted sesame oil

1 tablespoon minced fresh ginger

1 tablespoon minced garlic

1 teaspoon sugar

1 teaspoon agave nectar or honey

For Serving

1 teaspoon sesame seeds

25 g chopped spring onions

1. For the wings: Season the wings with the salt and pepper and place in the air fryer basket. Set the air fryer to 200°C for 20 minutes, turning the wings halfway through the cooking time. 2. Meanwhile, for the sauce: In a small bowl, combine the gochujang, mayonnaise, sesame oil, ginger, garlic, sugar, and agave; set aside. 3. As you near the 20-minute mark, use a meat thermometer to check the meat. When the wings reach 70°C, transfer them to a large bowl. Pour about half the sauce on the wings; toss to coat (serve the remaining sauce as a dip). 4. Return the wings to the air fryer basket and cook for 5 minutes, until the sauce has glazed. 5. Transfer the wings to a serving platter. Sprinkle with the sesame seeds and spring onions. Serve with the reserved sauce on the side for dipping.

Buffalo Crispy Chicken Strips

Prep time: 15 minutes | Cook time: 13 to 17 minutes per batch | Serves 4

90 g all-purpose flour	pepper
2 eggs	16 chicken breast strips, or 3
2 tablespoons water	large boneless, skinless chicken
120 g seasoned panko bread	breasts, cut into 1-inch strips
crumbs	Olive oil spray
2 teaspoons granulated garlic	60 ml Buffalo sauce, plus more
1 teaspoon salt	as needed
1 teaspoon freshly ground black	

1. Put the flour in a small bowl. 2. In another small bowl, whisk the eggs and the water. 3. In a third bowl, stir together the panko, granulated garlic, salt, and pepper. 4. Dip each chicken strip in the flour, in the egg, and in the panko mixture to coat. Press the crumbs onto the chicken with your fingers. 5. Insert the crisper plate into the basket and the basket into the unit. Preheat the unit by selecting AIR FRY, setting the temperature to 190°C, and setting the time to 3 minutes. Select START/STOP to begin. 6. Once the unit is preheated, place a parchment paper liner into the basket. Working in batches if needed, place the chicken strips into the basket. Do not stack unless using a wire rack for the second layer. Spray the top of the chicken with olive oil. 7. Select AIR FRY, set the temperature to 190°C, and set the time to 17 minutes. Select START/STOP to begin. 8. After 10 or 12 minutes, remove the basket, flip the chicken, and spray again with olive oil. Reinsert the basket to resume cooking. 9. When the cooking is complete, the chicken should be golden brown and crispy and a food thermometer inserted into the chicken should register 76°C. 10. Repeat steps 6, 7, and 8 with any remaining chicken. 11. Transfer the chicken to a large bowl. Drizzle the Buffalo sauce over the top of the cooked chicken, toss to coat, and serve.

Herbed Roast Chicken Breast

Prep time: 10 minutes | Cook time: 25 minutes | Serves 2 to 4

2 tablespoons salted butter or	½ teaspoon smoked paprika
ghee, at room temperature	¼ teaspoon black pepper
1 teaspoon dried Italian	2 bone-in, skin-on chicken
seasoning, crushed	breast halves (280 g each)
½ teaspoon kosher salt	Lemon wedges, for serving

1. In a small bowl, stir together the butter, Italian seasoning, salt, paprika, and pepper until thoroughly combined. 2. Using a small sharp knife, carefully loosen the skin on each chicken breast half, starting at the thin end of each. Very carefully separate the skin from the flesh, leaving the skin attached at the thick end of each breast. Divide the herb butter into quarters. Rub one-quarter of the butter onto the flesh of each breast. Fold and lightly press the skin back onto each breast. Rub the remaining butter onto the skin of each breast. 3. Place the chicken in the air fryer basket. Set the air fryer to (190°C for 25 minutes. Use a meat thermometer to ensure the chicken breasts have reached an internal temperature of 76°C. 4. Transfer the chicken to a cutting board. Lightly cover with aluminum foil and let rest for 5 to 10 minutes. 5. Serve with lemon wedges.

Buttermilk-Fried Drumsticks

Prep time: 10 minutes | Cook time: 25 minutes | Serves 2

1 egg	1 teaspoon salt
120 g buttermilk	¼ teaspoon ground black
90 g self-rising flour	pepper (to mix into coating)
90 g seasoned panko bread	4 chicken drumsticks, skin on
crumbs	Oil for misting or cooking spray

1. Beat together egg and buttermilk in shallow dish. 2. In a second shallow dish, combine the flour, panko crumbs, salt, and pepper. 3. Sprinkle chicken legs with additional salt and pepper to taste. 4. Dip legs in buttermilk mixture, then roll in panko mixture, pressing in crumbs to make coating stick. Mist with oil or cooking spray. 5. Spray the air fryer basket with cooking spray. 6. Cook drumsticks at 180°C for 10 minutes. Turn pieces over and cook an additional 10 minutes. 7. Turn pieces to check for browning. If you have any white spots that haven't begun to brown, spritz them with oil or cooking spray. Continue cooking for 5 more minutes or until crust is golden brown and juices run clear. Larger, meatier drumsticks will take longer to cook than small ones.

Yellow Curry Chicken Thighs with Peanuts

Prep time: 10 minutes | Cook time: 20 minutes | Serves 6

120 ml unsweetened full-fat	1 tablespoon minced garlic
coconut milk	1 teaspoon kosher salt
2 tablespoons yellow curry	450 g boneless, skinless chicken
paste	thighs, halved crosswise
1 tablespoon minced fresh	2 tablespoons chopped peanuts
ginger	

1. In a large bowl, stir together the coconut milk, curry paste, ginger, garlic, and salt until well blended. Add the chicken; toss well to coat. Marinate at room temperature for 30 minutes, or cover and refrigerate for up to 24 hours. 2. Preheat the air fryer to 190°C. 3. Place the chicken (along with marinade) in a baking pan. Place the pan in the air fryer basket. Bake for 20 minutes, turning the chicken halfway through the cooking time. Use a meat thermometer to ensure the chicken has reached an internal temperature of 76°C. 4. Sprinkle the chicken with the chopped peanuts and serve.

Chicken Legs with Leeks

Prep time: 30 minutes | Cook time: 18 minutes |

Serves 6

2 leeks, sliced	skinless
2 large-sized tomatoes, chopped	½ teaspoon smoked cayenne
3 cloves garlic, minced	pepper
½ teaspoon dried oregano	2 tablespoons olive oil
6 chicken legs, boneless and	A freshly ground nutmeg

1. In a mixing dish, thoroughly combine all ingredients, minus the leeks. Place in the refrigerator and let it marinate overnight. 2. Lay the leeks onto the bottom of the air fryer basket. Top with the chicken legs. 3. Roast chicken legs at (190ºC for 18 minutes, turning halfway through. Serve with hoisin sauce.

Crisp Paprika Chicken Drumsticks

Prep time: 5 minutes | Cook time: 22 minutes | Serves 2

2 teaspoons paprika	4 (140 g) chicken drumsticks,
1 teaspoon packed brown sugar	trimmed
1 teaspoon garlic powder	1 teaspoon vegetable oil
½ teaspoon dry mustard	1 scallion, green part only,
½ teaspoon salt	sliced thin on bias
Pinch pepper	

1. Preheat the air fryer to 200ºC. 2. Combine paprika, sugar, garlic powder, mustard, salt, and pepper in a bowl. Pat drumsticks dry with paper towels. Using metal skewer, poke 10 to 15 holes in skin of each drumstick. Rub with oil and sprinkle evenly with spice mixture. 3. Arrange drumsticks in air fryer basket, spaced evenly apart, alternating ends. Air fry until chicken is crisp and registers 90ºC, 22 to 25 minutes, flipping chicken halfway through cooking. 4. Transfer chicken to serving platter, tent loosely with aluminum foil, and let rest for 5 minutes. Sprinkle with scallion and serve.

Apricot-Glazed Turkey Tenderloin

Prep time: 20 minutes | Cook time: 30 minutes | Serves 4

Olive oil	mustard
80 g sugar-free apricot	680 g turkey breast tenderloin
preserves	Salt and freshly ground black
½ tablespoon spicy brown	pepper, to taste

1. Spray the air fryer basket lightly with olive oil. 2. In a small bowl, combine the apricot preserves and mustard to make a paste. 3. Season the turkey with salt and pepper. Spread the apricot paste all over the turkey. 4. Place the turkey in the air fryer basket and lightly spray with olive oil. 5. Air fry at 190ºC for 15 minutes. Flip the turkey over and lightly spray with olive oil. Air fry until the internal temperature reaches at least 80ºC, an additional 10 to 15 minutes. 6. Let the turkey rest for 10 minutes before slicing and serving.

Air Fried Chicken Wings with Buffalo Sauce

Prep time: 10 minutes | Cook time: 20 minutes |

Serves 6

16 chicken drumettes (party	1 teaspoon garlic powder
wings)	Ground black pepper, to taste
Chicken seasoning or rub, to	60 ml buffalo wings sauce
taste	Cooking spray

1. Preheat the air fryer to 200ºC. Spritz the air fryer basket with cooking spray. 2. Rub the chicken wings with chicken seasoning, garlic powder, and ground black pepper on a clean work surface. 3. Arrange the chicken wings in the preheated air fryer. Spritz with cooking spray. Air fry for 10 minutes or until lightly browned. Shake the basket halfway through. 4. Transfer the chicken wings in a large bowl, then pour in the buffalo wings sauce and toss to coat well. 5. Put the wings back to the air fryer and cook for an additional 7 minutes. 6. Serve immediately.

Korean Flavour Glazed Chicken Wings

Prep time: 10 minutes | Cook time: 25 minutes | Serves 4

Wings:	1 tablespoon minced garlic
900 g chicken wings	1 teaspoon agave nectar
1 teaspoon salt	2 packets Splenda
1 teaspoon ground black pepper	1 tablespoon sesame oil
Sauce:	For Garnish:
2 tablespoons gochujang	2 teaspoons sesame seeds
1 tablespoon mayonnaise	15 g chopped green onions
1 tablespoon minced ginger	

1. Preheat the air fryer to 200ºC. Line a baking pan with aluminum foil, then arrange the rack on the pan. 2. On a clean work surface, rub the chicken wings with salt and ground black pepper, then arrange the seasoned wings on the rack. 3. Air fry for 20 minutes or until the wings are well browned. Flip the wings halfway through. You may need to work in batches to avoid overcrowding. 4. Meanwhile, combine the ingredients for the sauce in a small bowl. Stir to mix well. Reserve half of the sauce in a separate bowl until ready to serve. 5. Remove the air fried chicken wings from the air fryer and toss with remaining half of the sauce to coat well. 6. Place the wings back to the air fryer and air fry for 5 more minutes or until the internal temperature of the wings reaches at least 76ºC. 7. Remove the wings from the air fryer and place on a large plate. Sprinkle with sesame seeds and green onions. Serve with reserved sauce.

Crunchy Chicken with Roasted Carrots

Prep time: 10 minutes | Cook time: 22 minutes | Serves 4

4 bone-in, skin-on chicken thighs	1 teaspoon sea salt, divided
2 carrots, cut into 2-inch pieces	2 teaspoons chopped fresh rosemary leaves
2 tablespoons extra-virgin olive oil	Cooking oil spray
2 teaspoons poultry spice	500 g cooked white rice

1. Brush the chicken thighs and carrots with olive oil. Sprinkle both with the poultry spice, salt, and rosemary. 2. Insert the crisper plate into the basket and the basket into the unit. Preheat the unit by selecting AIR FRY, setting the temperature to 200ºC, and setting the time to 3 minutes. Select START/STOP to begin. 3. Once the unit is preheated, spray the crisper plate with cooking oil. Place the carrots into the basket. Add the wire rack and arrange the chicken thighs on the rack. 4. Select AIR FRY, set the temperature to 200ºC, and set the time to 20 minutes. Select START/STOP to begin. 5. When the cooking is complete, check the chicken temperature. If a food thermometer inserted into the chicken registers 76ºC, remove the chicken from the air fryer, place it on a clean plate, and cover with aluminum foil to keep warm. Otherwise, resume cooking for 1 to 2 minutes longer. 6. The carrots can cook for 18 to 22 minutes and will be tender and caramelized; cooking time isn't as crucial for root vegetables. 7. Serve the chicken and carrots with the hot cooked rice.

Piri-Piri Chicken Thighs

Prep time: 5 minutes | Cook time: 25 minutes | Serves 4

60 ml piri-piri sauce	1 tablespoon extra-virgin olive oil
1 tablespoon freshly squeezed lemon juice	4 bone-in, skin-on chicken thighs, each weighing approximately 200 to 230 g
2 tablespoons brown sugar, divided	
2 cloves garlic, minced	½ teaspoon cornflour

1. To make the marinade, whisk together the piri-piri sauce, lemon juice, 1 tablespoon of brown sugar, and the garlic in a small bowl. While whisking, slowly pour in the oil in a steady stream and continue to whisk until emulsified. Using a skewer, poke holes in the chicken thighs and place them in a small glass dish. Pour the marinade over the chicken and turn the thighs to coat them with the sauce. Cover the dish and refrigerate for at least 15 minutes and up to 1 hour. 2. Preheat the air fryer to 190ºC. Remove the chicken thighs from the dish, reserving the marinade, and place them skin-side down in the air fryer basket. Air fry until the internal temperature reaches 76ºC, 15 to 20 minutes. 3. Meanwhile, whisk the remaining brown sugar and the cornflour into the marinade and microwave it on high power for 1 minute until it is bubbling and thickened to a glaze. 4. Once the chicken is cooked, turn the thighs over and brush them with the glaze. Air fry for a few additional minutes until the glaze browns and begins to char in spots. 5. Remove the chicken to a platter and serve with additional piri-piri sauce, if desired.

Chicken and Gruyère Cordon Bleu

Prep time: 15 minutes | Cook time: 15 minutes | Serves 4

4 chicken breast filets	Freshly ground black pepper, to taste
75 g chopped ham	
75 g grated Swiss cheese, or Gruyère cheese	½ teaspoon dried marjoram
	1 egg
30 g all-purpose flour	120 g panko bread crumbs
Pinch salt	Olive oil spray

1. Put the chicken breast filets on a work surface and gently press them with the palm of your hand to make them a bit thinner. Don't tear the meat. 2. In a small bowl, combine the ham and cheese. Divide this mixture among the chicken filets. Wrap the chicken around the filling to enclose it, using toothpicks to hold the chicken together. 3. In a shallow bowl, stir together the flour, salt, pepper, and marjoram. 4. In another bowl, beat the egg. 5. Spread the panko on a plate. 6. Dip the chicken in the flour mixture, in the egg, and in the panko to coat thoroughly. Press the crumbs into the chicken so they stick well. 7. Insert the crisper plate into the basket and the basket into the unit. Preheat the unit by selecting BAKE, setting the temperature to 190ºC, and setting the time to 3 minutes. Select START/STOP to begin. 8. Once the unit is preheated, spray the crisper plate with olive oil. Place the chicken into the basket and spray it with olive oil. 9. Select BAKE, set the temperature to 190ºC, and set the time to 15 minutes. Select START/STOP to begin. 10. When the cooking is complete, the chicken should be cooked through and a food thermometer inserted into the chicken should register 76ºC. Carefully remove the toothpicks and serve.

Buffalo Chicken Cheese Sticks

Prep time: 5 minutes | Cook time: 8 minutes | Serves 2

140 g shredded cooked chicken	cheese
60 ml buffalo sauce	1 large egg
220 g shredded Mozzarella	55 g crumbled feta

1. In a large bowl, mix all ingredients except the feta. Cut a piece of parchment to fit your air fryer basket and press the mixture into a ½-inch-thick circle. 2. Sprinkle the mixture with feta and place into the air fryer basket. 3. Adjust the temperature to 200ºC and air fry for 8 minutes. 4. After 5 minutes, flip over the cheese mixture. 5. Allow to cool 5 minutes before cutting into sticks. Serve warm.

Sweet Chili Spiced Chicken

Prep time: 10 minutes | Cook time: 43 minutes | Serves 4

Spice Rub:

2 tablespoons brown sugar

2 tablespoons paprika

1 teaspoon dry mustard powder

1 teaspoon chili powder

2 tablespoons coarse sea salt or

kosher salt

2 teaspoons coarsely ground black pepper

1 tablespoon vegetable oil

1 (1.6 kg) chicken, cut into 8 pieces

1. Prepare the spice rub by combining the brown sugar, paprika, mustard powder, chili powder, salt and pepper. Rub the oil all over the chicken pieces and then rub the spice mix onto the chicken, covering completely. This is done very easily in a zipper sealable bag. You can do this ahead of time and let the chicken marinate in the refrigerator, or just proceed with cooking right away. 2. Preheat the air fryer to 190ºC. 3. Air fry the chicken in two batches. Place the two chicken thighs and two drumsticks into the air fryer basket. Air fry at 190ºC for 10 minutes. Then, gently turn the chicken pieces over and air fry for another 10 minutes. Remove the chicken pieces and let them rest on a plate while you cook the chicken breasts. Air fry the chicken breasts, skin side down for 8 minutes. Turn the chicken breasts over and air fry for another 12 minutes. 4. Lower the temperature of the air fryer to 170ºC. Place the first batch of chicken on top of the second batch already in the basket and air fry for a final 3 minutes. 5. Let the chicken rest for 5 minutes and serve warm with some mashed potatoes and a green salad or vegetables.

Cheese-Encrusted Chicken Tenderloins with Peanuts

Prep time: 10 minutes | Cook time: 25 minutes | Serves 4

45 g grated Parmesan cheese

½ teaspoon garlic powder

1 teaspoon red pepper flakes

Sea salt and ground black pepper, to taste

2 tablespoons peanut oil

680 g chicken tenderloins

2 tablespoons peanuts, roasted and roughly chopped

Cooking spray

1. Preheat the air fryer to 180ºC. Spritz the air fryer basket with cooking spray. 2. Combine the Parmesan cheese, garlic powder, red pepper flakes, salt, black pepper, and peanut oil in a large bowl. Stir to mix well. 3. Dip the chicken tenderloins in the cheese mixture, then press to coat well. Shake the excess off. 4. Transfer the chicken tenderloins in the air fryer basket. Air fry for 12 minutes or until well browned. Flip the tenderloin halfway through. You may need to work in batches to avoid overcrowding. 5. Transfer the chicken tenderloins on a large plate and top with roasted peanuts before serving.

African Piri-Piri Chicken Drumsticks

Prep time: 30 minutes | Cook time: 20 minutes | Serves 2

Chicken:

1 tablespoon chopped fresh thyme leaves

1 tablespoon minced fresh ginger

1 small shallot, finely chopped

2 garlic cloves, minced

80 ml piri-piri sauce or hot sauce

3 tablespoons extra-virgin olive oil

Zest and juice of 1 lemon

1 teaspoon smoked paprika

½ teaspoon kosher salt

½ teaspoon black pepper

4 chicken drumsticks

Glaze:

2 tablespoons butter or ghee

1 teaspoon chopped fresh thyme leaves

1 garlic clove, minced

1 tablespoon piri-piri sauce

1 tablespoon fresh lemon juice

1. For the chicken: In a small bowl, stir together all the ingredients except the chicken. Place the chicken and the marinade in a gallon-size resealable plastic bag. Seal the bag and massage to coat. Refrigerate for at least 2 hours or up to 24 hours, turning the bag occasionally. 2. Place the chicken legs in the air fryer basket. Set the air fryer to 200ºC for 20 minutes, turning the chicken halfway through the cooking time. 3. Meanwhile, for the glaze: Melt the butter in a small saucepan over medium-high heat. Add the thyme and garlic. Cook, stirring, until the garlic just begins to brown, 1 to 2 minutes. Add the piri-piri sauce and lemon juice. Reduce the heat to medium-low and simmer for 1 to 2 minutes. 4. Transfer the chicken to a serving platter. Pour the glaze over the chicken. Serve immediately.

Peachy Chicken Chunks with Cherries

Prep time: 8 minutes | Cook time: 14 to 16 minutes | Serves 4

100 g peach preserves

1 teaspoon ground rosemary

½ teaspoon black pepper

½ teaspoon salt

½ teaspoon marjoram

1 teaspoon light olive oil

450 g boneless chicken breasts, cut in 1½-inch chunks

Oil for misting or cooking spray

1 (280 g) package frozen unsweetened dark cherries, thawed and drained

1. In a medium bowl, mix together peach preserves, rosemary, pepper, salt, marjoram, and olive oil. 2. Stir in chicken chunks and toss to coat well with the preserve mixture. 3. Spray the air fryer basket with oil or cooking spray and lay chicken chunks in basket. 4. Air fry at 200ºC for 7 minutes. Stir. Cook for 6 to 8 more minutes or until chicken juices run clear. 5. When chicken has cooked through, scatter the cherries over and cook for additional minute to heat cherries.

Easy Chicken Fingers

Prep time: 20 minutes | Cook time: 30 minutes |
Makes 12 chicken fingers

60 g all-purpose flour
240 g panko breadcrumbs
2 tablespoons rapeseed oil
1 large egg
3 boneless and skinless chicken

breasts, each cut into 4 strips
Kosher salt and freshly ground
black pepper, to taste
Cooking spray

1. Preheat the air fryer to 180ºC. Spritz the air fryer basket with cooking spray. 2. Pour the flour in a large bowl. Combine the panko and rapeseed oil on a shallow dish. Whisk the egg in a separate bowl. 3. Rub the chicken strips with salt and ground black pepper on a clean work surface, then dip the chicken in the bowl of flour. Shake the excess off and dunk the chicken strips in the bowl of whisked egg, then roll the strips over the panko to coat well. 4. Arrange 4 strips in the air fryer basket each time and air fry for 10 minutes or until crunchy and lightly browned. Flip the strips halfway through. Repeat with remaining ingredients. 5. Serve immediately.

Thai Chicken with Cucumber and Chili Salad

Prep time: 25 minutes | Cook time: 25 minutes | Serves 6

2 (570 g) small chickens,
giblets discarded
1 tablespoon fish sauce
6 tablespoons chopped fresh
coriander
2 teaspoons lime zest
1 teaspoon ground coriander
2 garlic cloves, minced
2 tablespoons packed light
brown sugar
2 teaspoons vegetable oil
Salt and ground black pepper,

to taste
1 English cucumber, halved
lengthwise and sliced thin
1 Thai chili, stemmed,
deseeded, and minced
2 tablespoons chopped dry-
roasted peanuts
1 small shallot, sliced thinly
1 tablespoon lime juice
Lime wedges, for serving
Cooking spray

1. Arrange a chicken on a clean work surface, remove the backbone with kitchen shears, then pound the chicken breast to flat. Cut the breast in half. Repeat with the remaining chicken. 2. Loose the breast and thigh skin with your fingers, then pat the chickens dry and pierce about 10 holes into the fat deposits of the chickens. Tuck the wings under the chickens. 3. Combine 2 teaspoons of fish sauce, coriander, lime zest, coriander, garlic, 4 teaspoons of sugar, 1 teaspoon of vegetable oil, ½ teaspoon of salt, and ⅛ teaspoon of ground black pepper in a small bowl. Stir to mix well. 4. Rub the fish sauce mixture under the breast and thigh skin of the game chickens, then let sit for 10 minutes to marinate. 5. Preheat the air fryer to 200ºC. Spritz the air fryer basket with cooking spray. 6. Arrange the marinated chickens in the preheated air fryer, skin side

down. 7. Air fry for 15 minutes, then gently turn the game hens over and air fry for 10 more minutes or until the skin is golden brown and the internal temperature of the chickens reads at least 76ºC. 8. Meanwhile, combine all the remaining ingredients, except for the lime wedges, in a large bowl and sprinkle with salt and black pepper. Toss to mix well. 9. Transfer the fried chickens on a large plate, then sit the salad aside and squeeze the lime wedges over before serving.

Fajita Chicken Strips

Prep time: 10 minutes | Cook time: 15 minutes | Serves 4

450 g boneless, skinless chicken
tenderloins, cut into strips
3 bell peppers, any color, cut
into chunks
1 onion, cut into chunks

1 tablespoon olive oil
1 tablespoon fajita seasoning
mix
Cooking spray

1. Preheat the air fryer to 190ºC. 2. In a large bowl, mix together the chicken, bell peppers, onion, olive oil, and fajita seasoning mix until completely coated. 3. Spray the air fryer basket lightly with cooking spray. 4. Place the chicken and vegetables in the air fryer basket and lightly spray with cooking spray. 5. Air fry for 7 minutes. Shake the basket and air fry for an additional 5 to 8 minutes, until the chicken is cooked through and the veggies are starting to char. 6. Serve warm.

Turkey and Cranberry Quesadillas

Prep time: 7 minutes | Cook time: 4 to 8 minutes |
Serves 4

6 low-sodium whole-wheat
tortillas
75 g shredded low-sodium low-
fat Swiss cheese
105 g shredded cooked low-
sodium turkey breast

2 tablespoons cranberry sauce
2 tablespoons dried cranberries
½ teaspoon dried basil
Olive oil spray, for spraying the
tortillas

1. Preheat the air fryer to 200ºC. 2. Put 3 tortillas on a work surface. 3. Evenly divide the Swiss cheese, turkey, cranberry sauce, and dried cranberries among the tortillas. Sprinkle with the basil and top with the remaining tortillas. 4. Spray the outsides of the tortillas with olive oil spray. 5. One at a time, air fry the quesadillas in the air fryer for 4 to 8 minutes, or until crisp and the cheese is melted. Cut into quarters and serve.

Classic Whole Chicken

Prep time: 5 minutes | Cook time: 50 minutes | Serves 4

Oil, for spraying

1 (1.8 kg) whole chicken, giblets removed

1 tablespoon olive oil

1 teaspoon paprika

½ teaspoon granulated garlic

½ teaspoon salt

½ teaspoon freshly ground black pepper

¼ teaspoon finely chopped fresh parsley, for garnish

1. Line the air fryer basket with parchment and spray lightly with oil. 2. Pat the chicken dry with paper towels. Rub it with the olive oil until evenly coated. 3. In a small bowl, mix together the paprika, garlic, salt, and black pepper and sprinkle it evenly over the chicken. 4. Place the chicken in the prepared basket, breast-side down. 5. Air fry at 180°C for 30 minutes, flip, and cook for another 20 minutes, or until the internal temperature reaches 76°C and the juices run clear. 6. Sprinkle with the parsley before serving.

Ham Chicken with Cheese

Prep time: 15 minutes | Cook time: 25 minutes | Serves 4

55 g unsalted butter, softened

115 g cream cheese, softened

1½ teaspoons Dijon mustard

2 tablespoons white wine vinegar

60 ml water

280 g shredded cooked chicken

115 g ham, chopped

115 g sliced Swiss or Provolone cheese

1. Preheat the air fryer to 190°C. Lightly coat a casserole dish that will fit in the air fryer, such as an 8-inch round pan, with olive oil and set aside. 2. In a large bowl and using an electric mixer, combine the butter, cream cheese, Dijon mustard, and vinegar. With the motor running at low speed, slowly add the water and beat until smooth. Set aside. 3. Arrange an even layer of chicken in the bottom of the prepared pan, followed by the ham. Spread the butter and cream cheese mixture on top of the ham, followed by the cheese slices on the top layer. Air fry for 20 to 25 minutes until warmed through and the cheese has browned.

Chapter 7 Beef, Pork, and Lamb

Chapter 7 Beef, Pork, and Lamb

Greek Stuffed Fillet

Prep time: 10 minutes | Cook time: 10 minutes | Serves 4

680 g venison or beef fillet, pounded to ¼ inch thick
3 teaspoons fine sea salt
1 teaspoon ground black pepper
60 g creamy goat cheese
120 ml crumbled feta cheese (about 60 g)
60 ml finely chopped onions
2 cloves garlic, minced
For Garnish/Serving (Optional):
Yellow/American mustard
Halved cherry tomatoes
Extra-virgin olive oil
Sprigs of fresh rosemary
Lavender flowers

1. Spray the air fryer basket with avocado oil. Preheat the air fryer to 204ºC. 2. Season the fillet on all sides with the salt and pepper. 3. In a medium-sized mixing bowl, combine the goat cheese, feta, onions, and garlic. Place the mixture in the center of the tenderloin. Starting at the end closest to you, tightly roll the tenderloin like a jelly roll. Tie the rolled tenderloin tightly with kitchen twine. 4. Place the meat in the air fryer basket and air fry for 5 minutes. Flip the meat over and cook for another 5 minutes, or until the internal temperature reaches 57ºC for medium-rare. 5. To serve, smear a line of yellow mustard on a platter, then place the meat next to it and add halved cherry tomatoes on the side, if desired. Drizzle with olive oil and garnish with rosemary sprigs and lavender flowers, if desired. 6. Best served fresh. Store leftovers in an airtight container in the fridge for 3 days. Reheat in a preheated 176ºC air fryer for 4 minutes, or until heated through.

Southern Chili

Prep time: 20 minutes | Cook time: 25 minutes | Serves 4

450 g beef mince (85% lean)
235 ml minced onion
1 (794 g) can tomato purée
1 (425 g) can diced tomatoes
1 (425 g) can red kidney beans, rinsed and drained
60 ml Chili seasoning

1. Preheat the air fryer to 204ºC. 2. In a baking pan, mix the mince and onion. Place the pan in the air fryer. 3. Cook for 4 minutes. Stir and cook for 4 minutes more until browned. Remove the pan from the fryer. Drain the meat and transfer to a large bowl. 4. Reduce the air fryer temperature to 176ºC. 5. To the bowl with the meat, add in the tomato purée, diced tomatoes, kidney beans, and Chili seasoning. Mix well. Pour the mixture into the baking pan. 6. Cook for 25 minutes, stirring every 10 minutes, until thickened.

Tomato and Bacon Zoodles

Prep time: 10 minutes | Cook time: 15 to 22 minutes | Serves 2

230 g sliced bacon
120 ml baby plum tomatoes
1 large courgette, spiralized
120 ml ricotta cheese
60 ml double/whipping cream
80 ml finely grated Parmesan cheese, plus more for serving
Sea salt and freshly ground black pepper, to taste

1. Set the air fryer to 204ºC. Arrange the bacon strips in a single layer in the air fryer basket—some overlapping is okay because the bacon will shrink, but cook in batches if needed. Air fry for 8 minutes. Flip the bacon strips and air fry for 2 to 5 minutes more, until the bacon is crisp. Remove the bacon from the air fryer. 2. Put the tomatoes in the air fryer basket and air fry for 3 to 5 minutes, until they are just starting to burst. Remove the tomatoes from the air fryer. 3. Put the courgette noodles in the air fryer and air fry for 2 to 4 minutes, to the desired doneness. 4. Meanwhile, combine the ricotta, cream, and Parmesan in a saucepan over medium-low heat. Cook, stirring often, until warm and combined. 5. Crumble the bacon. Place the courgette, bacon, and tomatoes in a bowl. Toss with the ricotta sauce. Season with salt and pepper, and sprinkle with additional Parmesan.

Beef and Tomato Sauce Meatloaf

Prep time: 15 minutes | Cook time: 25 minutes | Serves 4

680 g beef mince
235 ml tomato sauce
120 ml breadcrumbs
2 egg whites
120 ml grated Parmesan cheese
1 diced onion
2 tablespoons chopped parsley
2 tablespoons minced ginger
2 garlic cloves, minced
½ teaspoon dried basil
1 teaspoon cayenne pepper
Salt and ground black pepper, to taste
Cooking spray

1. Preheat the air fryer to 182ºC. Spritz a meatloaf pan with cooking spray. 2. Combine all the ingredients in a large bowl. Stir to mix well. 3. Pour the meat mixture in the prepared meatloaf pan and press with a spatula to make it firm. 4. Arrange the pan in the preheated air fryer and bake for 25 minutes or until the beef is well browned. 5. Serve immediately.

Beef Whirls

Prep time: 30 minutes | Cook time: 18 minutes | Serves 6

3 minute steaks (170 g each)
1 (450 g) bottle Italian dressing
235 ml Italian-style bread crumbs (or plain bread crumbs with Italian seasoning to taste)
120 ml grated Parmesan cheese

1 teaspoon dried basil
1 teaspoon dried oregano
1 teaspoon dried parsley
60 ml beef stock
1 to 2 tablespoons oil

1. In a large resealable bag, combine the steaks and Italian dressing. Seal the bag and refrigerate to marinate for 2 hours. 2. In a medium bowl, whisk the bread crumbs, cheese, basil, oregano, and parsley until blended. Stir in the beef stock. 3. Place the steaks on a cutting board and cut each in half so you have 6 equal pieces. Sprinkle with the bread crumb mixture. Roll up the steaks, jelly roll-style, and secure with toothpicks. 4. Preheat the air fryer to 204ºC. 5. Place 3 roll-ups in the air fryer basket. 6. Cook for 5 minutes. Flip the roll-ups and spritz with oil. Cook for 4 minutes more until the internal temperature reaches 64ºC. Repeat with the remaining roll-ups. Let rest for 5 to 10 minutes before serving.

Steak with Bell Pepper

Prep time: 30 minutes | Cook time: 20 to 23 minutes | Serves 6

60 ml avocado oil
60 ml freshly squeezed lime juice
2 teaspoons minced garlic
1 tablespoon chili powder
½ teaspoon ground cumin
Sea salt and freshly ground black pepper, to taste

450 g top rump steak or bavette or skirt steak, thinly sliced against the grain
1 red pepper, cored, seeded, and cut into ½-inch slices
1 green pepper, cored, seeded, and cut into ½-inch slices
1 large onion, sliced

1. In a small bowl or blender, combine the avocado oil, lime juice, garlic, chili powder, cumin, and salt and pepper to taste. 2. Place the sliced steak in a zip-top bag or shallow dish. Place the peppers and onion in a separate zip-top bag or dish. Pour half the marinade over the steak and the other half over the vegetables. Seal both bags and let the steak and vegetables marinate in the refrigerator for at least 1 hour or up to 4 hours. 3. Line the air fryer basket with an air fryer liner or aluminum foil. Remove the vegetables from their bag or dish and shake off any excess marinade. Set the air fryer to 204ºC. Place the vegetables in the air fryer basket and cook for 13 minutes. 4. Remove the steak from its bag or dish and shake off any excess marinade. Place the steak on top of the vegetables in the air fryer, and cook for 7 to 10 minutes or until an instant-read thermometer reads 49ºC for medium-rare (or cook to your desired doneness). 5. Serve with desired fixings, such as keto tortillas, lettuce, sour cream, avocado slices, shredded Cheddar cheese, and coriander.

Spicy Bavette Steak with Zhoug

Prep time: 30 minutes | Cook time: 8 minutes | Serves 4

Marinade and Steak:
120 ml dark beer or orange juice
60 ml fresh lemon juice
3 cloves garlic, minced
2 tablespoons extra-virgin olive oil
2 tablespoons Sriracha
2 tablespoons brown sugar
2 teaspoons ground cumin
2 teaspoons smoked paprika
1 tablespoon coarse or flaky salt
1 teaspoon black pepper

680 g bavette or skirt steak, trimmed and cut into 3 pieces
Zhoug:
235 ml packed fresh coriander leaves
2 cloves garlic, peeled
2 jalapeño or green chiles, stemmed and coarsely chopped
½ teaspoon ground cumin
¼ teaspoon ground coriander
¼ teaspoon coarse or flaky salt
2 to 4 tablespoons extra-virgin olive oil

1. For the marinade and steak: In a small bowl, whisk together the beer, lemon juice, garlic, olive oil, Sriracha, brown sugar, cumin, paprika, salt, and pepper. Place the steak in a large resealable plastic bag. Pour the marinade over the steak, seal the bag, and massage the steak to coat. Marinate in the refrigerator for 1 hour or up to 24 hours, turning the bag occasionally. 2. Meanwhile, for the zhoug: In a food processor, combine the coriander, garlic, jalapeños, cumin, coriander, and salt. Process until finely chopped. Add 2 tablespoons olive oil and pulse to form a loose paste, adding up to 2 tablespoons more olive oil if needed. Transfer the zhoug to a glass container. Cover and store in the refrigerator until 30 minutes before serving if marinating more than 1 hour. 3. Remove the steak from the marinade and discard the marinade. Place the steak in the air fryer basket and set the air fryer to 204ºC for 8 minutes. Use a meat thermometer to ensure the steak has reached an internal temperature of 64ºC (for medium). 4. Transfer the steak to a cutting board and let rest for 5 minutes. Slice the steak across the grain and serve with the zhoug.

Onion Pork Kebabs

Prep time: 22 minutes | Cook time: 18 minutes | Serves 3

2 tablespoons tomato purée
½ fresh green chilli, minced
⅓ teaspoon paprika
450 g pork mince
120 ml spring onions, finely chopped

3 cloves garlic, peeled and finely minced
1 teaspoon ground black pepper, or more to taste
1 teaspoon salt, or more to taste

1. Thoroughly combine all ingredients in a mixing dish. Then form your mixture into sausage shapes. 2. Cook for 18 minutes at 179ºC. Mound salad on a serving platter, top with air-fried kebabs and serve warm. Bon appétit!

Spinach and Mozzarella Steak Rolls

Prep time: 10 minutes | Cook time: 12 minutes |
Makes 8 rolls

1 (450 g) bavette or skirt steak, butterflied
8 (30 g, ¼-inch-thick) slices low-moisture Mozzarella or other melting cheese
235 ml fresh spinach leaves
½ teaspoon salt
¼ teaspoon ground black pepper

1. Place steak on a large plate. Place Mozzarella slices to cover steak, leaving 1-inch at the edges. Lay spinach leaves over cheese. Gently roll steak and tie with kitchen twine or secure with toothpicks. Carefully slice into eight pieces. Sprinkle each with salt and pepper. 2. Place rolls into ungreased air fryer basket, cut side up. Adjust the temperature to 204°C and air fry for 12 minutes. Steak rolls will be browned and cheese will be melted when done and have an internal temperature of at least 64°C for medium steak and 82°C for well-done steak. Serve warm.

Bacon, Cheese and Pear Stuffed Pork

Prep time: 10 minutes | Cook time: 24 minutes | Serves 3

4 slices bacon, chopped
1 tablespoon butter
120 ml finely diced onion
80 ml chicken stock
355 ml seasoned stuffing mix
1 egg, beaten
½ teaspoon dried thyme
½ teaspoon salt
⅛ teaspoon black pepper
1 pear, finely diced
80 ml crumbled blue cheese
3 boneless pork chops (2-inch thick)
Olive oil
Salt and freshly ground black pepper, to taste

1. Preheat the air fryer to 204°C. 2. Place the bacon into the air fryer basket and air fry for 6 minutes, stirring halfway through the cooking time. Remove the bacon and set it aside on a paper towel. Pour out the grease from the bottom of the air fryer. 3. Make the stuffing: Melt the butter in a medium saucepan over medium heat on the stovetop. Add the onion and sauté for a few minutes, until it starts to soften. Add the chicken stock and simmer for 1 minute. Remove the pan from the heat and add the stuffing mix. Stir until the stock has been absorbed. Add the egg, dried thyme, salt and freshly ground black pepper, and stir until combined. Fold in the diced pear and crumbled blue cheese. 4. Place the pork chops on a cutting board. Using the palm of your hand to hold the chop flat and steady, slice into the side of the pork chop to make a pocket in the center of the chop. Leave about an inch of chop uncut and make sure you don't cut all the way through the pork chop. Brush both sides of the pork chops with olive oil and season with salt and freshly ground black pepper. Stuff each pork chop with a third of the stuffing, packing the stuffing tightly inside the pocket. 5. Preheat the air fryer to 182°C. 6. Spray or brush the sides of the air fryer

basket with oil. Place the pork chops in the air fryer basket with the open stuffed edge of the pork chop facing the outside edges of the basket. 7. Air fry the pork chops for 18 minutes, turning the pork chops over halfway through the cooking time. When the chops are done, let them rest for 5 minutes and then transfer to a serving platter.

Greek Lamb Rack

Prep time: 5 minutes | Cook time: 10 minutes | Serves 4

60 ml freshly squeezed lemon juice
1 teaspoon oregano
2 teaspoons minced fresh rosemary
1 teaspoon minced fresh thyme
2 tablespoons minced garlic
Salt and freshly ground black pepper, to taste
2 to 4 tablespoons olive oil
1 lamb rib rack (7 to 8 ribs)

1. Preheat the air fryer to 182°C. 2. In a small mixing bowl, combine the lemon juice, oregano, rosemary, thyme, garlic, salt, pepper, and olive oil and mix well. 3. Rub the mixture over the lamb, covering all the meat. Put the rack of lamb in the air fryer. Roast for 10 minutes. Flip the rack halfway through. 4. After 10 minutes, measure the internal temperature of the rack of lamb reaches at least 64°C. 5. Serve immediately.

Pork Chops with Caramelized Onions

Prep time: 20 minutes | Cook time: 23 to 34 minutes | Serves 4

4 bone-in pork chops (230 g each)
1 to 2 tablespoons oil
2 tablespoons Cajun seasoning,
divided
1 brown onion, thinly sliced
1 green pepper, thinly sliced
2 tablespoons light brown sugar

1. Spritz the pork chops with oil. Sprinkle 1 tablespoon of Cajun seasoning on one side of the chops. 2. Preheat the air fryer to 204°C. Line the air fryer basket with parchment paper and spritz the parchment with oil. 3. Place 2 pork chops, spice-side up, on the paper. 4. Cook for 4 minutes. Flip the chops, sprinkle with the remaining 1 tablespoon of Cajun seasoning, and cook for 4 to 8 minutes more until the internal temperature reaches 64°C, depending on the chops' thickness. Remove and keep warm while you cook the remaining 2 chops. Set the chops aside. 5. In a baking pan, combine the onion, pepper, and brown sugar, stirring until the vegetables are coated. Place the pan in the air fryer basket and cook for 4 minutes. 6. Stir the vegetables. Cook for 3 to 6 minutes more to your desired doneness. Spoon the vegetable mixture over the chops to serve.

Lamb Chops with Horseradish Sauce

Prep time: 30 minutes | Cook time: 13 minutes | Serves 4

Lamb:
4 lamb loin chops
2 tablespoons vegetable oil
1 clove garlic, minced
½ teaspoon coarse or flaky salt
½ teaspoon black pepper
Horseradish Cream Sauce:

120 ml mayonnaise
1 tablespoon Dijon mustard
1 to 1½ tablespoons grated horseradish
2 teaspoons sugar
Vegetable oil spray

1. For the lamb: Brush the lamb chops with the oil, rub with the garlic, and sprinkle with the salt and pepper. Marinate at room temperature for 30 minutes. 2. Meanwhile, for the sauce: In a medium bowl, combine the mayonnaise, mustard, horseradish, and sugar. Stir until well combined. Set aside half of the sauce for serving. 3. Spray the air fryer basket with vegetable oil spray and place the chops in the basket. Set the air fryer to 164°C for 10 minutes, turning the chops halfway through the cooking time. 4. Remove the chops from the air fryer and add to the bowl with the horseradish sauce, turning to coat with the sauce. Place the chops back in the air fryer basket. Set the air fryer to 204°C for 3 minutes. Use a meat thermometer to ensure the meat has reached an internal temperature of 64°C (for medium-rare). 5. Serve the chops with the reserved horseradish sauce.

Bean and Beef Meatball Taco Pizza

Prep time: 10 minutes | Cook time: 7 to 9 minutes per batch | Serves 4

180 ml refried beans (from a 450 g can)
120 ml salsa
10 frozen precooked beef meatballs, thawed and sliced
1 jalapeño pepper, sliced

4 whole-wheat pitta breads
235 ml shredded chilli cheese
120 ml shredded Monterey Jack or Cheddar cheese
Cooking oil spray
80 ml sour cream

1. In a medium bowl, stir together the refried beans, salsa, meatballs, and jalapeño. 2. Insert the crisper plate into the basket and the basket into the unit. Preheat the unit by selecting BAKE, setting the temperature to 192°C, and setting the time to 3 minutes. Select START/STOP to begin. 3. Top the pittas with the refried bean mixture and sprinkle with the cheeses. 4. Once the unit is preheated, spray the crisper plate with cooking oil. Working in batches, place the pizzas into the basket. Select BAKE, set the temperature to 192°C, and set the time to 9 minutes. Select START/STOP to begin. 5. After about 7 minutes, check the pizzas. They are done when the cheese is melted and starts to brown. If not ready, resume cooking. 6. When the cooking is complete, top each pizza with a dollop of sour cream and serve warm.

Asian Glazed Meatballs

Prep time: 15 minutes | Cook time: 10 minutes per batch | Serves 4 to 6

1 large shallot, finely chopped
2 cloves garlic, minced
1 tablespoon grated fresh ginger
2 teaspoons fresh thyme, finely chopped
355 ml brown mushrooms, very finely chopped (a food processor works well here)
2 tablespoons soy sauce
Freshly ground black pepper, to

taste
450 g beef mince
230 g pork mince
3 egg yolks
235 ml Thai sweet chili sauce (spring roll sauce)
60 ml toasted sesame seeds
2spring onionspring onions, sliced

1. Combine the shallot, garlic, ginger, thyme, mushrooms, soy sauce, freshly ground black pepper, beef and pork mince, and egg yolks in a bowl and mix the ingredients together. Gently shape the mixture into 24 balls, about the size of a golf ball. 2. Preheat the air fryer to 192°C. 3. Working in batches, air fry the meatballs for 8 minutes, turning the meatballs over halfway through the cooking time. Drizzle some of the Thai sweet chili sauce on top of each meatball and return the basket to the air fryer, air frying for another 2 minutes. Reserve the remaining Thai sweet chili sauce for serving. 4. As soon as the meatballs are done, sprinkle with toasted sesame seeds and transfer them to a serving platter. Scatter the spring onionspring onions around and serve warm.

Mongolian-Style Beef

Prep time: 10 minutes | Cook time: 10 minutes | Serves 4

Oil, for spraying
60 ml cornflour
450 g bavette or skirt steak, thinly sliced
180 ml packed light brown sugar
120 ml soy sauce

2 teaspoons toasted sesame oil
1 tablespoon minced garlic
½ teaspoon ground ginger
120 ml water
Cooked white rice or ramen noodles, for serving

1. Line the air fryer basket with parchment and spray lightly with oil. 2. Place the cornflour in a bowl and dredge the steak until evenly coated. Shake off any excess cornflour. 3. Place the steak in the prepared basket and spray lightly with oil. 4. Roast at 200°C for 5 minutes, flip, and cook for another 5 minutes. 5. In a small saucepan, combine the brown sugar, soy sauce, sesame oil, garlic, ginger, and water and bring to a boil over medium-high heat, stirring frequently. Remove from the heat. 6. Transfer the meat to the sauce and toss until evenly coated. Let sit for about 5 minutes so the steak absorbs the flavors. Serve with white rice or ramen noodles.

Blackened Cajun Pork Roast

Prep time: 20 minutes | Cook time: 33 minutes | Serves 4

900 g bone-in pork loin roast	120 ml diced celery
2 tablespoons oil	120 ml diced green pepper
60 ml Cajun seasoning	1 tablespoon minced garlic
120 ml diced onion	

1. Cut 5 slits across the pork roast. Spritz it with oil, coating it completely. Evenly sprinkle the Cajun seasoning over the pork roast. 2. In a medium bowl, stir together the onion, celery, green pepper, and garlic until combined. Set aside. 3. Preheat the air fryer to 182ºC. Line the air fryer basket with parchment paper. 4. Place the pork roast on the parchment and spritz with oil. 5. Cook for 5 minutes. Flip the roast and cook for 5 minutes more. Continue to flip and cook in 5-minute increments for a total cook time of 20 minutes. 6. Increase the air fryer temperature to 200ºC. 7. Cook the roast for 8 minutes more and flip. Add the vegetable mixture to the basket and cook for a final 5 minutes. Let the roast sit for 5 minutes before serving.

Smoky Pork Tenderloin

Prep time: 5 minutes | Cook time: 19 to 22 minutes | Serves 6

680 g pork tenderloin	1 teaspoon garlic powder
1 tablespoon avocado oil	1 teaspoon sea salt
1 teaspoon chili powder	1 teaspoon freshly ground black
1 teaspoon smoked paprika	pepper

1. Pierce the tenderloin all over with a fork and rub the oil all over the meat. 2. In a small dish, stir together the chili powder, smoked paprika, garlic powder, salt, and pepper. 3. Rub the spice mixture all over the tenderloin. 4. Set the air fryer to 204ºC. Place the pork in the air fryer basket and air fry for 10 minutes. Flip the tenderloin and cook for 9 to 12 minutes more, until an instant-read thermometer reads at least 64ºC. 5. Allow the tenderloin to rest for 5 minutes, then slice and serve.

Sweet and Spicy Country-Style Ribs

Prep time: 10 minutes | Cook time: 25 minutes | Serves 4

2 tablespoons brown sugar	1 teaspoon coarse or flaky salt
2 tablespoons smoked paprika	1 teaspoon black pepper
1 teaspoon garlic powder	¼ to ½ teaspoon cayenne
1 teaspoon onion granules	pepper
1 teaspoon mustard powder	680 g boneless pork steaks
1 teaspoon ground cumin	235 ml barbecue sauce

1. In a small bowl, stir together the brown sugar, paprika, garlic powder, onion granules, mustard powder, cumin, salt, black pepper, and cayenne. Mix until well combined. 2. Pat the ribs dry with a paper towel. Generously sprinkle the rub evenly over both sides of the ribs and rub in with your fingers. 3. Place the ribs in the air fryer basket. Set the air fryer to 176ºC for 15 minutes. Turn the ribs and brush with 120 ml of the barbecue sauce. Cook for an additional 10 minutes. Use a meat thermometer to ensure the pork has reached an internal temperature of 64ºC. 4. Serve with remaining barbecue sauce.

Air Fryer Chicken-Fried Steak

Prep time: 5 minutes | Cook time: 20 minutes | Serves 4

450 g beef braising steak	2 medium egg whites
700 ml low-fat milk, divided	235 ml gluten-free breadcrumbs
1 teaspoon dried thyme	120 ml coconut flour
1 teaspoon dried rosemary	1 tablespoon Cajun seasoning

1. In a bowl, marinate the steak in 475 ml of milk for 30 to 45 minutes. 2. Remove the steak from milk, shake off the excess liquid, and season with the thyme and rosemary. Discard the milk. 3. In a shallow bowl, beat the egg whites with the remaining 235 ml of milk. 4. In a separate shallow bowl, combine the breadcrumbs, coconut flour, and seasoning. 5. Dip the steak in the egg white mixture then dredge in the breadcrumb mixture, coating well. 6. Place the steak in the basket of an air fryer. 7. Set the air fryer to 200ºC, close, and cook for 10 minutes. 8. Open the air fryer, turn the steaks, close, and cook for 10 minutes. Let rest for 5 minutes.

Cheese Crusted Chops

Prep time: 10 minutes | Cook time: 12 minutes | Serves 4 to 6

¼ teaspoon pepper	1 teaspoon smoked paprika
½ teaspoons salt	2 beaten eggs
4 to 6 thick boneless pork chops	3 tablespoons grated Parmesan
235 ml pork scratching crumbs	cheese
¼ teaspoon chili powder	Cooking spray
½ teaspoons onion granules	

1. Preheat the air fryer to 205ºC. 2. Rub the pepper and salt on both sides of pork chops. 3. In a food processor, pulse pork scratchings into crumbs. Mix crumbs with chili powder, onion granules, and paprika in a bowl. 4. Beat eggs in another bowl. 5. Dip pork chops into eggs then into pork scratchings crumb mixture. 6. Spritz the air fryer basket with cooking spray and add pork chops to the basket. 7. Air fry for 12 minutes. 8. Serve garnished with the Parmesan cheese.

Sesame Beef Lettuce Tacos

Prep time: 30 minutes | Cook time: 8 to 10 minutes | Serves 4

60 ml soy sauce or tamari	450 g bavette or skirt steak
60 ml avocado oil	8 butterhead lettuce leaves
2 tablespoons cooking sherry	2 spring onions, sliced
1 tablespoon granulated sweetener	1 tablespoon toasted sesame seeds
1 tablespoon ground cumin	Hot sauce, for serving
1 teaspoon minced garlic	Lime wedges, for serving
Sea salt and freshly ground black pepper, to taste	Flaky sea salt (optional)

1. In a small bowl, whisk together the soy sauce, avocado oil, cooking sherry, sweetener, cumin, garlic, and salt and pepper to taste. 2. Place the steak in a shallow dish. Pour the marinade over the beef. Cover the dish with plastic wrap and let it marinate in the refrigerator for at least 2 hours or overnight. 3. Remove the flank steak from the dish and discard the marinade. 4. Set the air fryer to 204°C. Place the steak in the air fryer basket and air fry for 4 to 6 minutes. Flip the steak and cook for 4 minutes more, until an instant-read thermometer reads 49°C at the thickest part (or cook it to your desired doneness). Allow the steak to rest for 10 minutes, then slice it thinly against the grain. 5. Stack 2 lettuce leaves on top of each other and add some sliced meat. Top with spring onions and sesame seeds. Drizzle with hot sauce and lime juice, and finish with a little flaky salt (if using). Repeat with the remaining lettuce leaves and fillings.

Zesty London Broil

Prep time: 30 minutes | Cook time: 20 to 28 minutes | Serves 4 to 6

160 ml ketchup	2 tablespoons minced onion
60 ml honey	½ teaspoon paprika
60 ml olive oil	1 teaspoon salt
2 tablespoons apple cider vinegar	1 teaspoon freshly ground black pepper
2 tablespoons Worcestershire sauce	900 g bavette or skirt steak (about 1-inch thick)

1. Combine the ketchup, honey, olive oil, apple cider vinegar, Worcestershire sauce, minced onion, paprika, salt and pepper in a small bowl and whisk together. 2. Generously pierce both sides of the meat with a fork or meat tenderizer and place it in a shallow dish. Pour the marinade mixture over the steak, making sure all sides of the meat get coated with the marinade. Cover and refrigerate overnight. 3. Preheat the air fryer to 204°C. 4. Transfer the steak to the air fryer basket and air fry for 20 to 28 minutes, depending on how rare or well done you like your steak. Flip the steak over halfway through the cooking time. 5. Remove the steak from the air fryer and let it rest for five minutes on a cutting board. To serve, thinly slice the meat against the grain and transfer to a serving platter.

Honey-Baked Pork Loin

Prep time: 30 minutes | Cook time: 22 to 25 minutes | Serves 6

60 ml honey	1 teaspoon garlic powder
60 ml freshly squeezed lemon juice	1 (900 g) pork loin
2 tablespoons soy sauce	2 tablespoons vegetable oil

1. In a medium bowl, whisk together the honey, lemon juice, soy sauce, and garlic powder. Reserve half of the mixture for basting during cooking. 2. Cut 5 slits in the pork loin and transfer it to a resealable bag. Add the remaining honey mixture. Seal the bag and refrigerate to marinate for at least 2 hours. 3. Preheat the air fryer to 204°C. Line the air fryer basket with parchment paper. 4. Remove the pork from the marinade, and place it on the parchment. Spritz with oil, then baste with the reserved marinade. 5. Cook for 15 minutes. Flip the pork, baste with more marinade and spritz with oil again. Cook for 7 to 10 minutes more until the internal temperature reaches 64°C. Let rest for 5 minutes before serving.

Fajita Meatball Lettuce Wraps

Prep time: 10 minutes | Cook time: 10 minutes | Serves 4

450 g beef mince (85% lean)	½ teaspoon chili powder
120 ml salsa, plus more for serving if desired	½ teaspoon ground cumin
60 ml chopped onions	1 clove garlic, minced
60 ml diced green or red peppers	For Serving (Optional):
1 large egg, beaten	8 leaves butterhead lettuce
1 teaspoon fine sea salt	Pico de gallo or salsa
	Lime slices

1. Spray the air fryer basket with avocado oil. Preheat the air fryer to 176°C. 2. In a large bowl, mix together all the ingredients until well combined. 3. Shape the meat mixture into eight 1-inch balls. Place the meatballs in the air fryer basket, leaving a little space between them. Air fry for 10 minutes, or until cooked through and no longer pink inside and the internal temperature reaches 64°C. 4. Serve each meatball on a lettuce leaf, topped with pico de gallo or salsa, if desired. Serve with lime slices if desired. 5. Store leftovers in an airtight container in the fridge for 3 days or in the freezer for up to a month. Reheat in a preheated 176°C air fryer for 4 minutes, or until heated through.

Pork Milanese

Prep time: 10 minutes | Cook time: 12 minutes | Serves 4

4 (1-inch) boneless pork chops
Fine sea salt and ground black
pepper, to taste
2 large eggs
180 ml pre-grated Parmesan

cheese
Chopped fresh parsley, for
garnish
Lemon slices, for serving

1. Spray the air fryer basket with avocado oil. Preheat the air fryer to 204°C. 2. Place the pork chops between 2 sheets of plastic wrap and pound them with the flat side of a meat tenderizer until they're ¼ inch thick. Lightly season both sides of the chops with salt and pepper. 3. Lightly beat the eggs in a shallow bowl. Divide the Parmesan cheese evenly between 2 bowls and set the bowls in this order: Parmesan, eggs, Parmesan. Dredge a chop in the first bowl of Parmesan, then dip it in the eggs, and then dredge it again in the second bowl of Parmesan, making sure both sides and all edges are well coated. Repeat with the remaining chops. 4. Place the chops in the air fryer basket and air fry for 12 minutes, or until the internal temperature reaches 64°C, flipping halfway through. 5. Garnish with fresh parsley and serve immediately with lemon slices. Store leftovers in an airtight container in the refrigerator for up to 3 days. Reheat in a preheated 200°C air fryer for 5 minutes, or until warmed through.

Parmesan-Crusted Steak

Prep time: 30 minutes | Cook time: 12 minutes | Serves 6

120 ml (1 stick) unsalted butter,
at room temperature
235 ml finely grated Parmesan
cheese
60 ml finely ground blanched

almond flour
680 g sirloin steak
Sea salt and freshly ground
black pepper, to taste

1. Place the butter, Parmesan cheese, and almond flour in a food processor. Process until smooth. Transfer to a sheet of parchment paper and form into a log. Wrap tightly in plastic wrap. Freeze for 45 minutes or refrigerate for at least 4 hours. 2. While the butter is chilling, season the steak liberally with salt and pepper. Let the steak rest at room temperature for about 45 minutes. 3. Place the grill pan or basket in your air fryer, set it to 204°C, and let it preheat for 5 minutes. 4. Working in batches, if necessary, place the steak on the grill pan and air fry for 4 minutes. Flip and cook for 3 minutes more, until the steak is brown on both sides. 5. Remove the steak from the air fryer and arrange an equal amount of the Parmesan butter on top of each steak. Return the steak to the air fryer and continue cooking for another 5 minutes, until an instant-read thermometer reads 49°C for medium-rare and the crust is golden brown (or to your desired doneness). 6. Transfer the cooked steak to a plate; let rest for 10 minutes before serving.

Kielbasa Sausage with Pineapple and Peppers

Prep time: 15 minutes | Cook time: 10 minutes | Serves 2 to 4

340 g kielbasa sausage, cut into
½-inch slices
1 (230 g) can pineapple chunks
in juice, drained
235 ml pepper chunks

1 tablespoon barbecue
seasoning
1 tablespoon soy sauce
Cooking spray

1. Preheat the air fryer to 200°C. Spritz the air fryer basket with cooking spray. 2. Combine all the ingredients in a large bowl. Toss to mix well. 3. Pour the sausage mixture in the preheated air fryer. 4. Air fry for 10 minutes or until the sausage is lightly browned and the pepper and pineapple are soft. Shake the basket halfway through. Serve immediately.

Pepper Steak

Prep time: 30 minutes | Cook time: 16 to 20 minutes | Serves 4

450 g minute steak, cut into
1-inch pieces
235 ml Italian dressing
355 ml beef stock
1 tablespoon soy sauce
½ teaspoon salt
¼ teaspoon freshly ground

black pepper
60 ml cornflour
235 ml thinly sliced pepper, any
color
235 ml chopped celery
1 tablespoon minced garlic
1 to 2 tablespoons oil

1. In a large resealable bag, combine the beef and Italian dressing. Seal the bag and refrigerate to marinate for 8 hours. 2. In a small bowl, whisk the beef stock, soy sauce, salt, and pepper until blended. 3. In another small bowl, whisk 60 ml water and the cornflour until dissolved. Stir the cornflour mixture into the beef stock mixture until blended. 4. Preheat the air fryer to 192°C. 5. Pour the stock mixture into a baking pan. Cook for 4 minutes. Stir and cook for 4 to 5 minutes more. Remove and set aside. 6. Increase the air fryer temperature to 204°C. Line the air fryer basket with parchment paper. 7. Remove the steak from the marinade and place it in a medium bowl. Discard the marinade. Stir in the pepper, celery, and garlic. 8. Place the steak and pepper mixture on the parchment. Spritz with oil. 9. Cook for 4 minutes. Shake the basket and cook for 4 to 7 minutes more, until the vegetables are tender and the meat reaches an internal temperature of 64°C. Serve with the gravy.

Pork Schnitzel with Dill Sauce

Prep time: 5 minutes | Cook time: 24 minutes | Serves 4 to 6

6 bonelesspork chops (about 680 g)
120 ml flour
1½ teaspoons salt
Freshly ground black pepper, to taste
2 eggs
120 ml milk
355 ml toasted fine bread crumbs
1 teaspoon paprika
3 tablespoons butter, melted

2 tablespoons vegetable or olive oil
lemon wedges
Dill Sauce:
235 ml chicken stock
1½ tablespoons cornflour
80 ml sour cream
1½ tablespoons chopped fresh dill
Salt and pepper, to taste

1. Trim the excess fat from the pork chops and pound each chop with a meat mallet between two pieces of plastic wrap until they are ½-inch thick. 2. Set up a dredging station. Combine the flour, salt, and black pepper in a shallow dish. Whisk the eggs and milk together in a second shallow dish. Finally, combine the bread crumbs and paprika in a third shallow dish. 3. Dip each flattened pork chop in the flour. Shake off the excess flour and dip each chop into the egg mixture. Finally dip them into the bread crumbs and press the bread crumbs onto the meat firmly. Place each finished chop on a baking sheet until they are all coated. 4. Preheat the air fryer to 204ºC. 5. Combine the melted butter and the oil in a small bowl and lightly brush both sides of the coated pork chops. Do not brush the chops too heavily or the breading will not be as crispy. 6. Air fry one schnitzel at a time for 4 minutes, turning it over halfway through the cooking time. Hold the cooked schnitzels warm on a baking pan in a 76ºC oven while you finish air frying the rest. 7. While the schnitzels are cooking, whisk the chicken stock and cornflour together in a small saucepan over medium-high heat on the stovetop. Bring the mixture to a boil and simmer for 2 minutes. Remove the saucepan from heat and whisk in the sour cream. Add the chopped fresh dill and season with salt and pepper. 8. Transfer the pork schnitzel to a platter and serve with dill sauce and lemon wedges.

Chapter 8 Fish and Seafood

Chapter 8 Fish and Seafood

Cod with Avocado

Prep time: 30 minutes | Cook time: 10 minutes | Serves 2

90 g shredded cabbage
60 ml full-fat sour cream
2 tablespoons full-fat
mayonnaise
20 g chopped pickled jalapeños
2 (85 g) cod fillets
1 teaspoon chilli powder

1 teaspoon cumin
½ teaspoon paprika
¼ teaspoon garlic powder
1 medium avocado, peeled,
pitted, and sliced
½ medium lime

1. In a large bowl, place cabbage, sour cream, mayonnaise, and jalapeños. Mix until fully coated. Let sit for 20 minutes in the refrigerator. 2. Sprinkle cod fillets with chilli powder, cumin, paprika, and garlic powder. Place each fillet into the air fryer basket. 3. Adjust the temperature to 188°C and set the timer for 10 minutes. 4. Flip the fillets halfway through the cooking time. When fully cooked, fish should have an internal temperature of at least 64°C. 5. To serve, divide slaw mixture into two serving bowls, break cod fillets into pieces and spread over the bowls, and top with avocado. Squeeze lime juice over each bowl. Serve immediately.

Garlicky Cod Fillets

Prep time: 10 minutes | Cook time: 10 to 12 minutes | Serves 4

1 teaspoon olive oil
4 cod fillets
¼ teaspoon fine sea salt
¼ teaspoon ground black
pepper, or more to taste
1 teaspoon cayenne pepper
8 g fresh Italian parsley,

coarsely chopped
120 ml milk
1 Italian pepper, chopped
4 garlic cloves, minced
1 teaspoon dried basil
½ teaspoon dried oregano

1. Lightly coat the sides and bottom of a baking dish with the olive oil. Set aside. 2. In a large bowl, sprinkle the fillets with salt, black pepper, and cayenne pepper. 3. In a food processor, pulse the remaining ingredients until smoothly puréed. 4. Add the purée to the bowl of fillets and toss to coat, then transfer to the prepared baking dish. 5. Preheat the air fryer to 192°C. 6. Put the baking dish in the air fryer basket and bake for 10 to 12 minutes, or until the fish flakes when pressed lightly with a fork. 7. Remove from the basket and serve warm.

Tandoori Prawns

Prep time: 25 minutes | Cook time: 6 minutes | Serves 4

455 g jumbo raw prawns (21 to
25 count), peeled and deveined
1 tablespoon minced fresh
ginger
3 cloves garlic, minced
5 g chopped fresh coriander or
parsley, plus more for garnish
1 teaspoon ground turmeric

1 teaspoon garam masala
1 teaspoon smoked paprika
1 teaspoon kosher or coarse sea
salt
½ to 1 teaspoon cayenne pepper
2 tablespoons olive oil (for
Paleo) or melted ghee
2 teaspoons fresh lemon juice

1. In a large bowl, combine the prawns, ginger, garlic, coriander, turmeric, garam masala, paprika, salt, and cayenne. Toss well to coat. Add the oil or ghee and toss again. Marinate at room temperature for 15 minutes, or cover and refrigerate for up to 8 hours. 2. Place the prawns in a single layer in the air fryer basket. Set the air fryer to 164°C for 6 minutes. Transfer the prawns to a serving platter. Cover and let the prawns finish cooking in the residual heat, about 5 minutes. 3. Sprinkle the prawns with the lemon juice and toss to coat. Garnish with additional cilantro and serve.

Catfish Bites

Prep time: 15 minutes | Cook time: 20 minutes | Serves 4

Olive or vegetable oil, for
spraying
455 g catfish fillets, cut into
2-inch pieces
235 ml buttermilk

70 g cornmeal
30 g plain flour
2 teaspoons Creole seasoning
120 ml yellow mustard

1. Line the air fryer basket with baking paper and spray lightly with oil. 2. Place the catfish pieces and buttermilk in a zip-top plastic bag, seal, and refrigerate for about 10 minutes. 3. In a shallow bowl, mix together the cornmeal, flour, and Creole seasoning. 4. Remove the catfish from the bag and pat dry with a paper towel. 5. Spread the mustard on all sides of the catfish, then dip them in the cornmeal mixture until evenly coated. 6. Place the catfish in the prepared basket. You may need to work in batches, depending on the size of your air fryer. Spray lightly with oil. 7. Air fry at 204°C for 10 minutes, flip carefully, spray with oil, and cook for another 10 minutes. Serve immediately.

Parmesan-Crusted Hake with Garlic Sauce

Prep time: 5 minutes | Cook time: 10 minutes | Serves 3

Fish:
6 tablespoons mayonnaise
1 tablespoon fresh lime juice
1 teaspoon Dijon mustard
150 g grated Parmesan cheese
Salt, to taste
¼ teaspoon ground black
pepper, or more to taste

3 hake fillets, patted dry
Nonstick cooking spray
Garlic Sauce:
60 ml plain Greek yogurt
2 tablespoons olive oil
2 cloves garlic, minced
½ teaspoon minced tarragon
leaves

1. Preheat the air fryer to 202ºC. 2. Mix the mayo, lime juice, and mustard in a shallow bowl and whisk to combine. In another shallow bowl, stir together the grated Parmesan cheese, salt, and pepper. 3. Dredge each fillet in the mayo mixture, then roll them in the cheese mixture until they are evenly coated on both sides. 4. Spray the air fryer basket with nonstick cooking spray. Arrange the fillets in the basket and air fry for 10 minutes, or until the fish flakes easily with a fork. Flip the fillets halfway through the cooking time. 5. Meanwhile, in a small bowl, whisk all the ingredients for the sauce until well incorporated. 6. Serve the fish warm alongside the sauce.

Fish Taco Bowl

Prep time: 10 minutes | Cook time: 12 minutes | Serves 4

½ teaspoon salt
¼ teaspoon garlic powder
¼ teaspoon ground cumin
4 cod fillets, 110 g each
360 g finely shredded green

cabbage
735 g mayonnaise
¼ teaspoon ground black
pepper
20 g chopped pickled jalapeños

1. Sprinkle salt, garlic powder, and cumin over cod and place into ungreased air fryer basket. Adjust the temperature to 176ºC and air fry for 12 minutes, turning fillets halfway through cooking. Cod will flake easily and have an internal temperature of at least 64ºC when done. 2. In a large bowl, toss cabbage with mayonnaise, pepper, and jalapeños until fully coated. Serve cod warm over cabbage slaw on four medium plates.

Crab Cakes with Bell Peppers

Prep time: 5 minutes | Cook time: 10 minutes | Serves 4

230 g jumbo lump crab meat
1 egg, beaten
Juice of ½ lemon
50 g bread crumbs
35 g diced green bell pepper

35 g diced red bell pepper
60 g mayonnaise
1 tablespoon Old Bay seasoning
1 teaspoon plain flour
Cooking spray

1. Preheat the air fryer to 190ºC. 2. Make the crab cakes: Place all the ingredients except the flour and oil in a large bowl and stir until well incorporated. 3. Divide the crab mixture into four equal portions and shape each portion into a patty with your hands. Top each patty with a sprinkle of ¼ teaspoon of flour. 4. Arrange the crab cakes in the air fryer basket and spritz them with cooking spray. 5. Air fry for 10 minutes, flipping the crab cakes halfway through, or until they are cooked through. 6. Divide the crab cakes among four plates and serve.

Tandoori-Spiced Salmon and Potatoes

Prep time: 10 minutes | Cook time: 28 minutes | Serves 2

455 g Fingerling or new
potatoes
2 tablespoons vegetable oil,
divided
Kosher or coarse sea salt and
freshly ground black pepper, to
taste

1 teaspoon ground turmeric
1 teaspoon ground cumin
1 teaspoon ground ginger
½ teaspoon smoked paprika
¼ teaspoon cayenne pepper
2 (170 g) skin-on salmon fillets

1. Preheat the air fryer to 192ºC. 2. In a bowl, toss the potatoes with 1 tablespoon of the oil until evenly coated. Season with salt and pepper. Transfer the potatoes to the air fryer and air fry for 20 minutes. 3. Meanwhile, in a bowl, combine the remaining 1 tablespoon oil, the turmeric, cumin, ginger, paprika, and cayenne. Add the salmon fillets and turn in the spice mixture until fully coated all over. 4. After the potatoes have cooked for 20 minutes, place the salmon fillets, skin-side up, on top of the potatoes, and continue cooking until the potatoes are tender, the salmon is cooked, and the salmon skin is slightly crisp. 5. Transfer the salmon fillets to two plates and serve with the potatoes while both are warm.

Lemony Salmon

Prep time: 30 minutes | Cook time: 10 minutes | Serves 4

680 g salmon steak
½ teaspoon grated lemon zest
Freshly cracked mixed
peppercorns, to taste
80 ml lemon juice
Fresh chopped chives, for

garnish
120 ml dry white wine, or apple
cider vinegar
½ teaspoon fresh coriander,
chopped
Fine sea salt, to taste

1. To prepare the marinade, place all ingredients, except for salmon steak and chives, in a deep pan. Bring to a boil over medium-high flame until it has reduced by half. Allow it to cool down. 2. After that, allow salmon steak to marinate in the refrigerator approximately 40 minutes. Discard the marinade and transfer the fish steak to the preheated air fryer. 3. Air fry at 204ºC for 9 to 10 minutes. To finish, brush hot fish steaks with the reserved marinade, garnish with fresh chopped chives, and serve right away!

Sea Bass with Roasted Root Vegetables

Prep time: 10 minutes | Cook time: 15 minutes | Serves 4

1 carrot, diced small	4 sea bass fillets
1 parsnip, diced small	½ teaspoon onion powder
1 swede, diced small	2 garlic cloves, minced
60 ml olive oil	1 lemon, sliced, plus additional
1 teaspoon salt, divided	wedges for serving

1. Preheat the air fryer to 192ºC. 2. In a small bowl, toss the carrot, parsnip, and swede with olive oil and 1 teaspoon salt. 3. Lightly season the sea bass with the remaining 1 teaspoon of salt and the onion powder, then place it into the air fryer basket in a single layer. 4. Spread the garlic over the top of each fillet, then cover with lemon slices. 5. Pour the prepared vegetables into the basket around and on top of the fish. Roast for 15 minutes. 6. Serve with additional lemon wedges if desired.

Lime Lobster Tails

Prep time: 10 minutes | Cook time: 6 minutes | Serves 4

4 lobster tails, peeled	½ teaspoon dried basil
2 tablespoons lime juice	½ teaspoon coconut oil, melted

1. Mix lobster tails with lime juice, dried basil, and coconut oil. 2. Put the lobster tails in the air fryer and cook at 192ºC for 6 minutes.

Apple Cider Mussels

Prep time: 10 minutes | Cook time: 2 minutes | Serves 5

900 g mussels, cleaned and de-bearded	1 teaspoon ground cumin
1 teaspoon onion powder	1 tablespoon avocado oil
	60 ml apple cider vinegar

1. Mix mussels with onion powder, ground cumin, avocado oil, and apple cider vinegar. 2. Put the mussels in the air fryer and cook at 202ºC for 2 minutes.

Roasted Salmon Fillets

Prep time: 5 minutes | Cook time: 10 minutes | Serves 2

2 (230 g) skin-on salmon fillets, 1½ inches thick	Salt and pepper, to taste
1 teaspoon vegetable oil	Vegetable oil spray

1. Preheat the air fryer to 204ºC. 2. Make foil sling for air fryer basket by folding 1 long sheet of aluminum foil so it is 4 inches wide. Lay sheet of foil widthwise across basket, pressing foil into and up sides of basket. Fold excess foil as needed so that edges of foil are flush with top of basket. Lightly spray foil and basket with vegetable oil spray. 3. Pat salmon dry with paper towels, rub with oil, and season with salt and pepper. Arrange fillets skin side down on sling in prepared basket, spaced evenly apart. Air fry salmon until center is still translucent when checked with the tip of a paring knife and registers 52ºC (for medium-rare), 10 to 14 minutes, using sling to rotate fillets halfway through cooking. 4. Using the sling, carefully remove salmon from air fryer. Slide fish spatula along underside of fillets and transfer to individual serving plates, leaving skin behind. Serve.

Foil-Packet Lobster Tail

Prep time: 15 minutes | Cook time: 12 minutes | Serves 2

2 lobster tails, 170 g each halved	½ teaspoon Old Bay seasoning
2 tablespoons salted butter, melted	Juice of ½ medium lemon
	1 teaspoon dried parsley

1. Place the two halved tails on a sheet of aluminum foil. Drizzle with butter, Old Bay seasoning, and lemon juice. 2. Seal the foil packets, completely covering tails. Place into the air fryer basket. 3. Adjust the temperature to 192ºC and air fry for 12 minutes. 4. Once done, sprinkle with dried parsley and serve immediately.

Fish Sandwich with Tartar Sauce

Prep time: 10 minutes | Cook time: 17 minutes | Serves 2

Tartar Sauce:	Fish:
115 g mayonnaise	2 tablespoons plain flour
2 tablespoons onion granules	1 egg, lightly beaten
1 dill pickle spear, finely chopped	120 g panko
2 teaspoons pickle juice	2 teaspoons lemon pepper
¼ teaspoon salt	2 tilapia fillets
⅛ teaspoon ground black pepper	Cooking spray
	2 soft sub rolls

1. Preheat the air fryer to 204ºC. 2. In a small bowl, combine the mayonnaise, onion granules, pickle, pickle juice, salt, and pepper. 3. Whisk to combine and chill in the refrigerator while you make the fish. 4. Place a baking paper liner in the air fryer basket. 5. Scoop the flour out onto a plate; set aside. 6. Put the beaten egg in a medium shallow bowl. 7. On another plate, mix to combine the panko and lemon pepper. 8. Dredge the tilapia fillets in the flour, then dip in the egg, and then press into the panko mixture. 9. Place the prepared fillets on the liner in the air fryer in a single layer. 10. Spray lightly with cooking spray and air fry for 8 minutes. Carefully flip the fillets, spray with more cooking spray, and air fry for an additional 9 minutes, until golden and crispy. 11. Place each cooked fillet in a sub roll, top with a little bit of tartar sauce, and serve.

Steamed Cod with Garlic and Swiss Chard

Prep time: 5 minutes | Cook time: 12 minutes | Serves 4

1 teaspoon salt
½ teaspoon dried oregano
½ teaspoon dried thyme
½ teaspoon garlic powder
4 cod fillets

½ white onion, thinly sliced
135 g Swiss chard, washed, stemmed, and torn into pieces
60 ml olive oil
1 lemon, quartered

1. Preheat the air fryer to 192°C. 2. In a small bowl, whisk together the salt, oregano, thyme, and garlic powder. 3. Tear off four pieces of aluminum foil, with each sheet being large enough to envelop one cod fillet and a quarter of the vegetables. 4. Place a cod fillet in the middle of each sheet of foil, then sprinkle on all sides with the spice mixture. 5. In each foil packet, place a quarter of the onion slices and 30 g Swiss chard, then drizzle 1 tablespoon olive oil and squeeze ¼ lemon over the contents of each foil packet. 6. Fold and seal the sides of the foil packets and then place them into the air fryer basket. Steam for 12 minutes. 7. Remove from the basket, and carefully open each packet to avoid a steam burn.

Creamy Haddock

Prep time: 10 minutes | Cook time: 8 minutes | Serves 4

455 g haddock fillet
1 teaspoon cayenne pepper
1 teaspoon salt

1 teaspoon coconut oil
120 ml heavy cream

1. Grease a baking pan with coconut oil. 2. Then put haddock fillet inside and sprinkle it with cayenne pepper, salt, and heavy cream. Put the baking pan in the air fryer basket and cook at 192°C for 8 minutes.

Classic Fish Sticks with Tartar Sauce

Prep time: 10 minutes | Cook time: 12 to 15 minutes | Serves 4

680 g cod fillets, cut into 1-inch strips
1 teaspoon salt
½ teaspoon freshly ground black pepper
2 eggs
70 g almond flour
20 g grated Parmesan cheese
Tartar Sauce:

120 ml sour cream
120 ml mayonnaise
3 tablespoons chopped dill pickle
2 tablespoons capers, drained and chopped
½ teaspoon dried dill
1 tablespoon dill pickle liquid (optional)

1. Preheat the air fryer to 204°C. 2. Season the cod with the salt and black pepper; set aside. 3. In a shallow bowl, lightly beat the eggs. In a second shallow bowl, combine the almond flour and Parmesan cheese. Stir until thoroughly combined. 4. Working with a few pieces at a time, dip the fish into the egg mixture followed by the flour mixture. Press lightly to ensure an even coating. 5. Working in batches if necessary, arrange the fish in a single layer in the air fryer basket and spray lightly with olive oil. Pausing halfway through the cooking time to turn the fish, air fry for 12 to 15 minutes, until the fish flakes easily with a fork. Let sit in the basket for a few minutes before serving with the tartar sauce. 6. To make the tartar sauce: In a small bowl, combine the sour cream, mayonnaise, pickle, capers, and dill. If you prefer a thinner sauce, stir in the pickle liquid.

Sole and Cauliflower Fritters

Prep time: 5 minutes | Cook time: 24 minutes | Serves 2

230 g sole fillets
230 g mashed cauliflower
75 g red onion, chopped
1 bell pepper, finely chopped
1 egg, beaten
2 garlic cloves, minced
2 tablespoons fresh parsley, chopped

1 tablespoon olive oil
1 tablespoon coconut aminos or tamari
½ teaspoon scotch bonnet pepper, minced
½ teaspoon paprika
Salt and white pepper, to taste
Cooking spray

1. Preheat the air fryer to 202°C. Spray the air fryer basket with cooking spray. 2. Place the sole fillets in the basket and air fry for 10 minutes, flipping them halfway through. 3. When the fillets are done, transfer them to a large bowl. Mash the fillets into flakes. Add the remaining ingredients and stir to combine. 4. Make the fritters: Scoop out 2 tablespoons of the fish mixture and shape into a patty about ½ inch thick with your hands. Repeat with the remaining fish mixture. 5. Arrange the patties in the air fryer basket and bake for 14 minutes, flipping the patties halfway through, or until they are golden brown and cooked through. 6. Cool for 5 minutes and serve on a plate.

Italian Baked Cod

Prep time: 5 minutes | Cook time: 12 minutes | Serves 4

4 cod fillets, 170 g each
2 tablespoons salted butter, melted
1 teaspoon Italian seasoning

¼ teaspoon salt
120 ml tomato-based pasta sauce

1. Place cod into an ungreased round nonstick baking dish. Pour butter over cod and sprinkle with Italian seasoning and salt. Top with pasta sauce. 2. Place dish into air fryer basket. Adjust the temperature to 176°C and bake for 12 minutes. Fillets will be lightly browned, easily flake, and have an internal temperature of at least 64°C when done. Serve warm.

Tuna Steak

Prep time: 10 minutes | Cook time: 12 minutes | Serves 4

455 g tuna steaks, boneless and cubed	1 tablespoon avocado oil
1 tablespoon mustard	1 tablespoon apple cider vinegar

1. Mix avocado oil with mustard and apple cider vinegar. 2. Then brush tuna steaks with mustard mixture and put in the air fryer basket. 3. Cook the fish at 182ºC for 6 minutes per side.

Scallops and Spinach with Cream Sauce

Prep time: 5 minutes | Cook time: 10 minutes | Serves 2

Vegetable oil spray	180 ml heavy cream
280 g frozen spinach, thawed and drained	1 tablespoon tomato paste
8 jumbo sea scallops	1 tablespoon chopped fresh basil
Kosher or coarse sea salt, and black pepper, to taste	1 teaspoon minced garlic

1. Spray a baking pan with vegetable oil spray. Spread the thawed spinach in an even layer in the bottom of the pan. 2. Spray both sides of the scallops with vegetable oil spray. Season lightly with salt and pepper. Arrange the scallops on top of the spinach. 3. In a small bowl, whisk together the cream, tomato paste, basil, garlic, ½ teaspoon salt, and ½ teaspoon pepper. Pour the sauce over the scallops and spinach. 4. Place the pan in the air fryer basket. Set the air fryer to 176ºC for 10 minutes. Use a meat thermometer to ensure the scallops have an internal temperature of 56ºC.

Crab Cakes with Sriracha Mayonnaise

Prep time: 15 minutes | Cook time: 10 minutes | Serves 4

Sriracha Mayonnaise:	40 g diced celery
230 g mayonnaise	455 g lump crab meat
1 tablespoon Sriracha	1 teaspoon Old Bay seasoning
1½ teaspoons freshly squeezed lemon juice	1 egg
Crab Cakes:	1½ teaspoons freshly squeezed lemon juice
1 teaspoon extra-virgin olive oil	200 g panko bread crumbs, divided
40 g finely diced red bell pepper	
40 g diced onion	Vegetable oil, for spraying

1. Mix the mayonnaise, Sriracha, and lemon juice in a small bowl. Place ⅓ of the mixture in a separate bowl to form the base of the crab cakes. Cover the remaining Sriracha mayonnaise and refrigerate. (This will become dipping sauce for the crab cakes once they are cooked.) 2. Heat the olive oil in a heavy-bottomed, medium skillet over medium-high heat. Add the bell pepper, onion, and celery and sauté for 3 minutes. Transfer the vegetables to the bowl with the reserved ⅔ of Sriracha mayonnaise. Mix in the crab, Old Bay seasoning, egg, and lemon juice. Add 120 g of the panko. Form the crab mixture into 8 cakes. Dredge the cakes in the remaining panko, turning to coat. Place on a baking sheet. Cover and refrigerate for at least 1 hour and up to 8 hours. 3. Preheat the air fryer to 192ºC. Spray the air fryer basket with oil. Working in batches as needed so as not to overcrowd the basket, place the chilled crab cakes in a single layer in the basket. Spray the crab cakes with oil. Bake until golden brown, 8 to 10 minutes, carefully turning halfway through cooking. Remove to a platter and keep warm. Repeat with the remaining crab cakes as needed. Serve the crab cakes immediately with Sriracha mayonnaise dipping sauce.

Fried Catfish with Dijon Sauce

Prep time: 20 minutes | Cook time: 7 minutes | Serves 4

4 tablespoons butter, melted	4 catfish fillets, 110g each
2 teaspoons Worcestershire sauce, divided	Cooking spray
1 teaspoon lemon pepper	120 ml sour cream
120 g panko bread crumbs	1 tablespoon Dijon mustard

1. In a shallow bowl, stir together the melted butter, 1 teaspoon of Worcestershire sauce, and the lemon pepper. Place the bread crumbs in another shallow bowl. 2. One at a time, dip both sides of the fillets in the butter mixture, then the bread crumbs, coating thoroughly. 3. Preheat the air fryer to 150ºC. Line the air fryer basket with baking paper. 4. Place the coated fish on the baking paper and spritz with oil. 5. Bake for 4 minutes. Flip the fish, spritz it with oil, and bake for 3 to 6 minutes more, depending on the thickness of the fillets, until the fish flakes easily with a fork. 6. In a small bowl, stir together the sour cream, Dijon, and remaining 1 teaspoon of Worcestershire sauce. This sauce can be made 1 day in advance and refrigerated before serving. Serve with the fried fish.

Prawns with Smoky Tomato Dressing

Prep time: 5 minutes | Cook time: 8 minutes | Serves 2

3 tablespoons mayonnaise	salt
1 tablespoon ketchup	455 g large raw prawns (21 to 25 count), peeled (tails left on) and deveined
1 tablespoon minced garlic	
1 teaspoon Sriracha	
½ teaspoon smoked paprika	Vegetable oil spray
½ teaspoon kosher or coarse sea	50 g chopped spring onions

1. In a large bowl, combine the mayonnaise, ketchup, garlic, Sriracha, paprika, and salt. Add the prawns and toss to coat with the sauce. 2. Spray the air fryer basket with vegetable oil spray. Place the prawns in the basket. Set the air fryer to 176ºC for 8 minutes, tossing and spraying the prawns with vegetable oil spray halfway through the cooking time. 3. Sprinkle with the chopped spring onions before serving.

Chapter 9 Snacks and Appetizers

Chapter 9 Snacks and Appetizers

Sausage Balls with Cheese

Prep time: 10 minutes | Cook time: 10 to 11 minutes | Serves 8

340 g mild sausage meat	85 g soft white cheese, at room
355 ml baking mix	temperature
240 ml shredded mild Cheddar	1 to 2 tablespoons olive oil
cheese	

1. Preheat the air fryer to 164ºC. Line the air fryer basket with parchment paper. 2. Mix together the ground sausage, baking mix, Cheddar cheese, and soft white cheese in a large bowl and stir to incorporate. 3. Divide the sausage mixture into 16 equal portions and roll them into 1-inch balls with your hands. 4. Arrange the sausage balls on the parchment, leaving space between each ball. You may need to work in batches to avoid overcrowding. 5. Brush the sausage balls with the olive oil. Bake for 10 to 11 minutes, shaking the basket halfway through, or until the balls are firm and lightly browned on both sides. 6. Remove from the basket to a plate and repeat with the remaining balls. 7. Serve warm.

Shrimp Pirogues

Prep time: 15 minutes | Cook time: 4 to 5 minutes | Serves 8

340 g small, peeled, and	1 teaspoon dried dill weed,
deveined raw shrimp	crushed
85 g soft white cheese, room	Salt, to taste
temperature	4 small hothouse cucumbers,
2 tablespoons natural yoghurt	each approximately 6 inches
1 teaspoon lemon juice	long

1. Pour 4 tablespoons water in bottom of air fryer drawer. 2. Place shrimp in air fryer basket in single layer and air fry at 200ºC for 4 to 5 minutes, just until done. Watch carefully because shrimp cooks quickly, and overcooking makes it tough. 3. Chop shrimp into small pieces, no larger than ½ inch. Refrigerate while mixing the remaining ingredients. 4. With a fork, mash and whip the soft white cheese until smooth. 5. Stir in the yoghurt and beat until smooth. Stir in lemon juice, dill weed, and chopped shrimp. 6. Taste for seasoning. If needed, add ¼ to ½ teaspoon salt to suit your taste. 7. Store in refrigerator until serving time. 8. When ready to serve, wash and dry cucumbers and split them lengthwise. Scoop out the seeds and turn cucumbers upside down on paper towels to drain

for 10 minutes. 9. Just before filling, wipe centres of cucumbers dry. Spoon the shrimp mixture into the pirogues and cut in half crosswise. Serve immediately.

Garlic Edamame

Prep time: 5 minutes | Cook time: 10 minutes | Serves 4

Olive oil	¼ teaspoon freshly ground
1 (454 g) bag frozen edamame	black pepper
in pods	½ teaspoon red pepper flakes
½ teaspoon salt	(optional)
½ teaspoon garlic salt	

1. Spray the air fryer basket lightly with olive oil. 2. In a medium bowl, add the frozen edamame and lightly spray with olive oil. Toss to coat. 3. In a small bowl, mix together the salt, garlic salt, black pepper, and red pepper flakes (if using). Add the mixture to the edamame and toss until evenly coated. 4. Place half the edamame in the air fryer basket. Do not overfill the basket. 5. Air fry at 192ºC for 5 minutes. Shake the basket and cook until the edamame is starting to brown and get crispy, 3 to 5 more minutes. 6. Repeat with the remaining edamame and serve immediately.

Stuffed Fried Mushrooms

Prep time: 20 minutes | Cook time: 10 to 11 minutes | Serves 10

120 ml panko breadcrumbs	1 (227 g) package soft white
½ teaspoon freshly ground	cheese, at room temperature
black pepper	20 cremini or button
½ teaspoon onion powder	mushrooms, stemmed
½ teaspoon cayenne pepper	1 to 2 tablespoons oil

1. In a medium bowl, whisk the breadcrumbs, black pepper, onion powder, and cayenne until blended. 2. Add the soft white cheese and mix until well blended. Fill each mushroom top with 1 teaspoon of the soft white cheese mixture 3. Preheat the air fryer to 182ºC. Line the air fryer basket with a piece of parchment paper. 4. Place the mushrooms on the parchment and spritz with oil. 5. Cook for 5 minutes. Shake the basket and cook for 5 to 6 minutes more until the filling is firm and the mushrooms are soft.

Cheesy Steak Fries

Prep time: 5 minutes | Cook time: 20 minutes | Serves 5

1 (794 g) bag frozen steak fries
Cooking spray
Salt and pepper, to taste
120 ml beef gravy

240 ml shredded Mozzarella cheese
2 spring onions, green parts only, chopped

1. Preheat the air fryer to 204°C. 2. Place the frozen steak fries in the air fryer. Air fry for 10 minutes. Shake the basket and spritz the fries with cooking spray. Sprinkle with salt and pepper. Air fry for an additional 8 minutes. 3. Pour the beef gravy into a medium, microwave-safe bowl. Microwave for 30 seconds, or until the gravy is warm. 4. Sprinkle the fries with the cheese. Air fry for an additional 2 minutes, until the cheese is melted. 5. Transfer the fries to a serving dish. Drizzle the fries with gravy and sprinkle the spring onions on top for a green garnish. Serve.

Peppery Chicken Meatballs

Prep time: 5 minutes | Cook time: 13 to 20 minutes | Makes 16 meatballs

2 teaspoons olive oil
60 ml minced onion
60 ml minced red pepper
2 vanilla wafers, crushed

1 egg white
½ teaspoon dried thyme
230 g minced chicken breast

1. Preheat the air fryer to 188°C. 2. In a baking pan, mix the olive oil, onion, and red pepper. Put the pan in the air fryer. Air fry for 3 to 5 minutes, or until the vegetables are tender. 3. In a medium bowl, mix the cooked vegetables, crushed wafers, egg white, and thyme until well combined 4. Mix in the chicken, gently but thoroughly, until everything is combined. 5. Form the mixture into 16 meatballs and place them in the air fryer basket. Air fry for 10 to 15 minutes, or until the meatballs reach an internal temperature of 74°C on a meat thermometer. 6. Serve immediately.

Garlicky and Cheesy French Fries

Prep time: 5 minutes | Cook time: 20 to 25 minutes | Serves 4

3 medium russet or Maris Piper potatoes, rinsed, dried, and cut into thin wedges or classic fry shapes
2 tablespoons extra-virgin olive oil
1 tablespoon granulated garlic

80 ml grated Parmesan cheese
½ teaspoon salt
¼ teaspoon freshly ground black pepper
Cooking oil spray
2 tablespoons finely chopped fresh parsley (optional)

1. In a large bowl combine the potato wedges or fries and the olive oil. Toss to coat. 2. Sprinkle the potatoes with the granulated garlic,

Parmesan cheese, salt, and pepper, and toss again. 3. Insert the crisper plate into the basket and the basket into the unit. Preheat the unit by selecting AIR FRY, setting the temperature to 204°C, and setting the time to 3 minutes. Select START/STOP to begin. 4. Once the unit is preheated, spray the crisper plate with cooking oil. Place the potatoes into the basket. 5. Select AIR FRY, set the temperature to 204°C, and set the time to 20 to 25 minutes. Select START/STOP to begin. 6. After about 10 minutes, remove the basket and shake it so the fries at the bottom come up to the top. Reinsert the basket to resume cooking. 7. When the cooking is complete, top the fries with the parsley (if using) and serve hot.

Lemony Pear Chips

Prep time: 15 minutes | Cook time: 9 to 13 minutes | Serves 4

2 firm Bosc or Anjou pears, cut crosswise into ⅛-inch-thick slices
1 tablespoon freshly squeezed

lemon juice
½ teaspoon ground cinnamon
⅛ teaspoon ground cardamom

1. Preheat the air fryer to 192°C. 2. Separate the smaller stem-end pear rounds from the larger rounds with seeds. Remove the core and seeds from the larger slices. Sprinkle all slices with lemon juice, cinnamon, and cardamom. 3. Put the smaller chips into the air fryer basket. Air fry for 3 to 5 minutes, or until light golden brown, shaking the basket once during cooking. Remove from the air fryer. 4. Repeat with the larger slices, air frying for 6 to 8 minutes, or until light golden brown, shaking the basket once during cooking. 5. Remove the chips from the air fryer. Cool and serve or store in an airtight container at room temperature up for to 2 days.

Mozzarella Arancini

Prep time: 5 minutes | Cook time: 8 to 11 minutes | Makes 16 arancini

475 ml cooked rice, cooled
2 eggs, beaten
355 ml panko breadcrumbs, divided
120 ml grated Parmesan cheese

2 tablespoons minced fresh basil
16 ¾-inch cubes Mozzarella cheese
2 tablespoons olive oil

1. Preheat the air fryer to 204°C. 2. In a medium bowl, combine the rice, eggs, 120 ml of the breadcrumbs, Parmesan cheese, and basil. Form this mixture into 16 1½-inch balls. 3. Poke a hole in each of the balls with your finger and insert a Mozzarella cube. Form the rice mixture firmly around the cheese. 4. On a shallow plate, combine the remaining 240 ml of the breadcrumbs with the olive oil and mix well. Roll the rice balls in the breadcrumbs to coat. 5. Air fry the arancini in batches for 8 to 11 minutes or until golden brown. 6. Serve hot.

Spicy Tortilla Chips

Prep time: 5 minutes | Cook time: 8 to 12 minutes | Serves 4

½ teaspoon ground cumin	Pinch cayenne pepper
½ teaspoon paprika	8 (6-inch) corn tortillas, each
½ teaspoon chilli powder	cut into 6 wedges
½ teaspoon salt	Cooking spray

1. Preheat the air fryer to 192°C. Lightly spritz the air fryer basket with cooking spray. 2. Stir together the cumin, paprika, chilli powder, salt, and pepper in a small bowl. 3. Working in batches, arrange the tortilla wedges in the air fryer basket in a single layer. Lightly mist them with cooking spray. Sprinkle some seasoning mixture on top of the tortilla wedges. 4. Air fry for 4 to 6 minutes, shaking the basket halfway through, or until the chips are lightly browned and crunchy. 5. Repeat with the remaining tortilla wedges and seasoning mixture. 6. Let the tortilla chips cool for 5 minutes and serve.

Goat Cheese and Garlic Crostini

Prep time: 3 minutes | Cook time: 5 minutes | Serves 4

1 wholemeal baguette	113 g goat cheese
60 ml olive oil	2 tablespoons fresh basil,
2 garlic cloves, minced	minced

1. Preheat the air fryer to 192°C. 2. Cut the baguette into ½-inch-thick slices. 3. In a small bowl, mix together the olive oil and garlic, then brush it over one side of each slice of bread. 4. Place the olive-oil-coated bread in a single layer in the air fryer basket and bake for 5 minutes. 5. Meanwhile, in a small bowl, mix together the goat cheese and basil. 6. Remove the toast from the air fryer, then spread a thin layer of the goat cheese mixture over the top of each piece and serve.

Vegetable Pot Stickers

Prep time: 12 minutes | Cook time: 11 to 18 minutes | Makes 12 pot stickers

240 ml shredded red cabbage	2 garlic cloves, minced
60 ml chopped button	2 teaspoons grated fresh ginger
mushrooms	12 gyoza/pot sticker wrappers
60 ml grated carrot	2½ teaspoons olive oil, divided
2 tablespoons minced onion	

1. In a baking pan, combine the red cabbage, mushrooms, carrot, onion, garlic, and ginger. Add 1 tablespoon of water. Place in the air fryer and air fry at 188°C for 3 to 6 minutes, until the vegetables are crisp-tender. Drain and set aside. 2. Working one at a time, place the pot sticker wrappers on a work surface. Top each wrapper with a scant 1 tablespoon of the filling. Fold half of the wrapper over the other half to form a half circle. Dab one edge with water and press both edges together. 3. To another pan, add 1¼ teaspoons of olive oil. Put half of the pot stickers, seam-side up, in the pan. Air fry for 5 minutes, or until the bottoms are light golden brown. Add 1 tablespoon of water and return the pan to the air fryer. 4. Air fry for 4 to 6 minutes more, or until hot. Repeat with the remaining pot stickers, remaining 1¼ teaspoons of oil, and another tablespoon of water. Serve immediately.

Dark Chocolate and Cranberry Granola Bars

Prep time: 5 minutes | Cook time: 15 minutes | Serves 6

475 ml certified gluten-free	3 tablespoons unsweetened
quick oats	shredded coconut
2 tablespoons sugar-free dark	120 ml raw honey
chocolate chunks	1 teaspoon ground cinnamon
2 tablespoons unsweetened	⅛ teaspoon salt
dried cranberries	2 tablespoons olive oil

1. Preheat the air fryer to 182°C. Line an 8-by-8-inch baking dish with parchment paper that comes up the side so you can lift it out after cooking. 2. In a large bowl, mix together all of the ingredients until well combined. 3. Press the oat mixture into the pan in an even layer. 4. Place the pan into the air fryer basket and bake for 15 minutes. 5. Remove the pan from the air fryer and lift the granola cake out of the pan using the edges of the parchment paper. 6. Allow to cool for 5 minutes before slicing into 6 equal bars. 7. Serve immediately or wrap in plastic wrap and store at room temperature for up to 1 week.

Crispy Cajun Dill Pickle Chips

Prep time: 5 minutes | Cook time: 10 minutes | Makes 16 slices

60 ml plain flour	2 large dill pickles, sliced into 8
120 ml panko breadcrumbs	rounds each
1 large egg, beaten	Cooking spray
2 teaspoons Cajun seasoning	

1. Preheat the air fryer to 200°C. 2. Place the plain flour, panko breadcrumbs, and egg into 3 separate shallow bowls, then stir the Cajun seasoning into the flour. 3. Dredge each pickle chip in the flour mixture, then the egg, and finally the breadcrumbs. Shake off any excess, then place each coated pickle chip on a plate. 4. Spritz the air fryer basket with cooking spray, then place 8 pickle chips in the basket and air fry for 5 minutes, or until crispy and golden brown. Repeat this process with the remaining pickle chips. 5. Remove the chips and allow to slightly cool on a wire rack before serving.

Greek Yoghurt Devilled Eggs

Prep time: 15 minutes | Cook time: 15 minutes | Serves 4

4 eggs
60 ml non-fat plain Greek yoghurt
1 teaspoon chopped fresh dill
⅛ teaspoon salt

⅛ teaspoon paprika
⅛ teaspoon garlic powder
Chopped fresh parsley, for garnish

1. Preheat the air fryer to 127ºC. 2. Place the eggs in a single layer in the air fryer basket and cook for 15 minutes. 3. Quickly remove the eggs from the air fryer and place them into a cold water bath. Let the eggs cool in the water for 10 minutes before removing and peeling them. 4. After peeling the eggs, cut them in half. 5. Spoon the yolk into a small bowl. Add the yoghurt, dill, salt, paprika, and garlic powder and mix until smooth. 6. Spoon or pipe the yolk mixture into the halved egg whites. Serve with a sprinkle of fresh parsley on top.

Beef and Mango Skewers

Prep time: 10 minutes | Cook time: 4 to 7 minutes | Serves 4

340 g beef sirloin tip, cut into 1-inch cubes
2 tablespoons balsamic vinegar
1 tablespoon olive oil
1 tablespoon honey

½ teaspoon dried marjoram
Pinch of salt
Freshly ground black pepper, to taste
1 mango

1. Preheat the air fryer to 200ºC. 2. Put the beef cubes in a medium bowl and add the balsamic vinegar, olive oil, honey, marjoram, salt, and pepper. Mix well, then massage the marinade into the beef with your hands. Set aside. 3. To prepare the mango, stand it on end and cut the skin off, using a sharp knife. Then carefully cut around the oval pit to remove the flesh. Cut the mango into 1-inch cubes. 4. Thread metal skewers alternating with three beef cubes and two mango cubes. 5. Roast the skewers in the air fryer basket for 4 to 7 minutes, or until the beef is browned and at least 63ºC. 6. Serve hot.

Crunchy Tex-Mex Tortilla Chips

Prep time: 5 minutes | Cook time: 5 minutes | Serves 4

Olive oil
½ teaspoon salt
½ teaspoon ground cumin
½ teaspoon chilli powder

½ teaspoon paprika
Pinch cayenne pepper
8 (6-inch) corn tortillas, each cut into 6 wedges

1. Spray fryer basket lightly with olive oil. 2. In a small bowl, combine the salt, cumin, chilli powder, paprika, and cayenne pepper. 3. Place the tortilla wedges in the air fryer basket in a single layer. Spray the tortillas lightly with oil and sprinkle with some of the seasoning mixture. You will need to cook the tortillas in batches. 4. Air fry at 192ºC for 2 to 3 minutes. Shake the basket and cook until the chips are light brown and crispy, an additional 2 to 3 minutes. Watch the chips closely so they do not burn.

Roasted Grape Dip

Prep time: 10 minutes | Cook time: 8 to 12 minutes | Serves 6

475 ml seedless red grapes, rinsed and patted dry
1 tablespoon apple cider vinegar
1 tablespoon honey

240 ml low-fat Greek yoghurt
2 tablespoons semi-skimmed milk
2 tablespoons minced fresh basil

1. In the air fryer basket, sprinkle the grapes with the cider vinegar and drizzle with the honey. Toss to coat. Roast the grapes at 192ºC for 8 to 12 minutes, or until shrivelled but still soft. Remove from the air fryer. 2. In a medium bowl, stir together the yoghurt and milk. 3. Gently blend in the grapes and basil. Serve immediately or cover and chill for 1 to 2 hours.

Five-Ingredient Falafel with Garlic-Yoghurt Sauce

Prep time: 5 minutes | Cook time: 15 minutes | Serves 4

Falafel:
1 (425 g) can chickpeas, drained and rinsed
120 ml fresh parsley
2 garlic cloves, minced
½ tablespoon ground cumin
1 tablespoon wholemeal flour

Salt
Garlic-Yoghurt Sauce:
240 ml non-fat plain Greek yoghurt
1 garlic clove, minced
1 tablespoon chopped fresh dill
2 tablespoons lemon juice

Make the Falafel: 1. Preheat the air fryer to 182ºC. 2. Put the chickpeas into a food processor. Pulse until mostly chopped, then add the parsley, garlic, and cumin and pulse for another 1 to 2 minutes, or until the ingredients are combined and turning into a dough. 3. Add the flour. Pulse a few more times until combined. The dough will have texture, but the chickpeas should be pulsed into small bits. 4. Using clean hands, roll the dough into 8 balls of equal size, then pat the balls down a bit so they are about ½-thick disks. 5. Spray the basket of the air fryer with olive oil cooking spray, then place the falafel patties in the basket in a single layer, making sure they don't touch each other. 6. Fry in the air fryer for 15 minutes. Make the garlic-yoghurt sauce 7. In a small bowl, combine the yoghurt, garlic, dill, and lemon juice. 8. Once the falafel is done cooking and nicely browned on all sides, remove them from the air fryer and season with salt. 9. Serve hot with a side of dipping sauce.

Stuffed Figs with Goat Cheese and Honey

Prep time: 5 minutes | Cook time: 10 minutes | Serves 4

8 fresh figs	1 tablespoon honey, plus more
57 g goat cheese	for serving
¼ teaspoon ground cinnamon	1 tablespoon olive oil

1. Preheat the air fryer to 182°C. Line an 8-by-8-inch baking dish with parchment paper that comes up the side so you can lift it out after cooking. 2. In a large bowl, mix together all of the ingredients until well combined. 3. Press the oat mixture into the pan in an even layer. 4. Place the pan into the air fryer basket and bake for 15 minutes. 5. Remove the pan from the air fryer and lift the granola cake out of the pan using the edges of the parchment paper. 6. Allow to cool for 5 minutes before slicing into 6 equal bars. 7. Serve immediately or wrap in plastic wrap and store at room temperature for up to 1 week.

Tangy Fried Pickle Spears

Prep time: 5 minutes | Cook time: 15 minutes | Serves 6

2 jars sweet and sour pickle	1 teaspoon sea salt
spears, patted dry	½ teaspoon shallot powder
2 medium-sized eggs	⅓ teaspoon chilli powder
80 ml milk	80 ml plain flour
1 teaspoon garlic powder	Cooking spray

1. Preheat the air fryer to 196°C. Spritz the air fryer basket with cooking spray. 2. In a bowl, beat together the eggs with milk. In another bowl, combine garlic powder, sea salt, shallot powder, chilli powder and plain flour until well blended. 3. One by one, roll the pickle spears in the powder mixture, then dredge them in the egg mixture. Dip them in the powder mixture a second time for additional coating. 4. Arrange the coated pickles in the prepared basket. Air fry for 15 minutes until golden and crispy, shaking the basket halfway through to ensure even cooking. 5. Transfer to a plate and let cool for 5 minutes before serving.

Air Fryer Popcorn with Garlic Salt

Prep time: 3 minutes | Cook time: 10 minutes | Serves 2

2 tablespoons olive oil	1 teaspoon garlic salt
60 ml popcorn kernels	

1. Preheat the air fryer to 192°C. 2. Tear a square of aluminium foil the size of the bottom of the air fryer and place into the air fryer. 3. Drizzle olive oil over the top of the foil, and then pour in the popcorn kernels. 4. Roast for 8 to 10 minutes, or until the popcorn stops popping. 5. Transfer the popcorn to a large bowl and sprinkle with garlic salt before serving.

Shrimp Toasts with Sesame Seeds

Prep time: 15 minutes | Cook time: 6 to 8 minutes | Serves 4 to 6

230 g raw shrimp, peeled and	1 to 2 teaspoons sriracha sauce
deveined	1 teaspoon soy sauce
1 egg, beaten	½ teaspoon toasted sesame oil
2 spring onions, chopped, plus	6 slices thinly sliced white
more for garnish	sandwich bread
2 tablespoons chopped fresh	120 ml sesame seeds
coriander	Cooking spray
2 teaspoons grated fresh ginger	Thai chilli sauce, for serving

1. Preheat the air fryer to 204°C. Spritz the air fryer basket with cooking spray. 2. In a food processor, add the shrimp, egg, spring onions, coriander, ginger, sriracha sauce, soy sauce and sesame oil, and pulse until chopped finely. You'll need to stop the food processor occasionally to scrape down the sides. Transfer the shrimp mixture to a bowl. 3. On a clean work surface, cut the crusts off the sandwich bread. Using a brush, generously brush one side of each slice of bread with shrimp mixture. 4. Place the sesame seeds on a plate. Press bread slices, shrimp-side down, into sesame seeds to coat evenly. Cut each slice diagonally into quarters. 5. Spread the coated slices in a single layer in the air fryer basket. 6. Air fry in batches for 6 to 8 minutes, or until golden and crispy. Flip the bread slices halfway through. Repeat with the remaining bread slices. 7. Transfer to a plate and let cool for 5 minutes. Top with the chopped spring onions and serve warm with Thai chilli sauce.

Polenta Fries with Chilli-Lime Mayo

Prep time: 10 minutes | Cook time: 28 minutes | Serves 4

Polenta Fries:	1 teaspoon chilli powder
2 teaspoons vegetable or olive	1 teaspoon chopped fresh
oil	coriander
¼ teaspoon paprika	¼ teaspoon ground cumin
450 g prepared polenta, cut into	Juice of ½ lime
3-inch × ½-inch strips	Salt and freshly ground black
Chilli-Lime Mayo:	pepper, to taste
120 ml mayonnaise	

1. Preheat the air fryer to 204°C. 2. Mix the oil and paprika in a bowl. Add the polenta strips and toss until evenly coated. 3. Transfer the polenta strips to the air fry basket and air fry for 28 minutes until the fries are golden brown, shaking the basket once during cooking. Season as desired with salt and pepper. 4. Meanwhile, whisk together all the ingredients for the chilli-lime mayo in a small bowl. 5. Remove the polenta fries from the air fryer to a plate and serve alongside the chilli-lime mayo as a dipping sauce.

Spiced Roasted Cashews

Prep time: 5 minutes | Cook time: 10 minutes | Serves 4

475 ml raw cashews

2 tablespoons olive oil

¼ teaspoon salt

¼ teaspoon chilli powder

⅛ teaspoon garlic powder

⅛ teaspoon smoked paprika

1. Preheat the air fryer to 182ºC. 2. In a large bowl, toss all of the ingredients together. 3. Pour the cashews into the air fryer basket and roast them for 5 minutes. Shake the basket, then cook for 5 minutes more. 4. Serve immediately.

Chapter 10 Vegetables and Sides

Chapter 10 Vegetables and Sides

Balsamic Brussels Sprouts

Prep time: 5 minutes | Cook time: 12 minutes | Serves 4

180 g trimmed and halved fresh
Brussels sprouts
2 tablespoons olive oil
¼ teaspoon salt
¼ teaspoon ground black

pepper
2 tablespoons balsamic vinegar
2 slices cooked sugar-free
bacon, crumbled

1. In a large bowl, toss Brussels sprouts in olive oil, then sprinkle with salt and pepper. Place into ungreased air fryer basket. Adjust the temperature to 192ºC and set the timer for 12 minutes, shaking the basket halfway through cooking. Brussels sprouts will be tender and browned when done. 2. Place sprouts in a large serving dish and drizzle with balsamic vinegar. Sprinkle bacon over top. Serve warm.

Chiles Rellenos with Red Chile Sauce

Prep time: 20 minutes | Cook time: 20 minutes | Serves 2

Peppers:
2 poblano peppers, rinsed and
dried
110 g thawed frozen or drained
canned corn kernels
1 spring onion, sliced
2 tablespoons chopped fresh
coriander
½ teaspoon coarse sea salt
¼ teaspoon black pepper
150 g grated Monterey Jack
cheese
Sauce:
3 tablespoons extra-virgin olive

oil
25 g finely chopped yellow
onion
2 teaspoons minced garlic
1 (170 g) can tomato paste
2 tablespoons ancho chili
powder
1 teaspoon dried oregano
1 teaspoon ground cumin
½ teaspoon coarse sea salt
470 ml chicken stock
2 tablespoons fresh lemon juice
Mexican crema or sour cream,
for serving

1. For the peppers: Place the peppers in the air fryer basket. Set the air fryer to 200ºC for 10 minutes, turning the peppers halfway through the cooking time, until their skins are charred. Transfer the peppers to a resealable plastic bag, seal, and set aside to steam for 5 minutes. Peel the peppers and discard the skins. Cut a slit down the centre of each pepper, starting at the stem and continuing to the tip. Remove the seeds, being careful not to tear the chile. 2. In a medium bowl, combine the corn, spring onion, coriander, salt, black pepper, and cheese; set aside. 3. Meanwhile, for the sauce:

In a large skillet, heat the olive oil over medium-high heat. Add the onion and cook, stirring, until tender, about 5 minutes. Add the garlic and cook, stirring, for 30 seconds. Stir in the tomato paste, chile powder, oregano, and cumin, and salt. Cook, stirring, for 1 minute. Whisk in the stock and lemon juice. Bring to a simmer and cook, stirring occasionally, while the stuffed peppers finish cooking. 4. Cut a slit down the centre of each poblano pepper, starting at the stem and continuing to the tip. Remove the seeds, being careful not to tear the chile. 5. Carefully stuff each pepper with half the corn mixture. Place the stuffed peppers in a baking pan. Place the pan in the air fryer basket. Set the air fryer to 200ºC for 10 minutes, or until the cheese has melted. 6. Transfer the stuffed peppers to a serving platter and drizzle with the sauce and some crema.

Gold Artichoke Hearts

Prep time: 15 minutes | Cook time: 8 minutes | Serves 4

12 whole artichoke hearts
packed in water, drained
60 g plain flour
1 egg

40 g panko bread crumbs
1 teaspoon Italian seasoning
Cooking oil spray

1. Squeeze any excess water from the artichoke hearts and place them on paper towels to dry. 2. Place the flour in a small bowl. 3. In another small bowl, beat the egg. 4. In a third small bowl, stir together the panko and Italian seasoning. 5. Dip the artichoke hearts in the flour, in the egg, and into the panko mixture until coated. 6. Insert the crisper plate into the basket and the basket into the unit. Preheat the unit by selecting AIR FRY, setting the temperature to 192ºC, and setting the time to 3 minutes. Select START/STOP to begin. 7. Once the unit is preheated, spray the crisper plate and the basket with cooking oil. Place the breaded artichoke hearts into the basket, stacking them if needed. 8. Select AIR FRY, set the temperature to 192ºC, and set the time to 8 minutes. Select START/STOP to begin. 9. After 4 minutes, use tongs to flip the artichoke hearts. I recommend flipping instead of shaking because the hearts are small, and this will help keep the breading intact. Re-insert the basket to resume cooking. 10. When the cooking is complete, the artichoke hearts should be deep golden brown and crisp. Cool for 5 minutes before serving.

Tingly Chili-Roasted Broccoli

Prep time: 5 minutes | Cook time: 10 minutes | Serves 2

340 g broccoli florets
2 tablespoons Asian hot chili oil
1 teaspoon ground Sichuan peppercorns (or black pepper)
2 garlic cloves, finely chopped

1 (2-inch) piece fresh ginger, peeled and finely chopped
coarse sea salt and freshly ground black pepper, to taste

1. In a bowl, toss together the broccoli, chili oil, Sichuan peppercorns, garlic, ginger, and salt and black pepper to taste. 2. Transfer to the air fryer and roast at 192ºC, shaking the basket halfway through, until lightly charred and tender, about 10 minutes. Remove from the air fryer and serve warm.

Tahini-Lemon Kale

Prep time: 5 minutes | Cook time: 15 minutes | Serves 2 to 4

60 g tahini
60 ml fresh lemon juice
2 tablespoons olive oil
1 teaspoon sesame seeds
½ teaspoon garlic powder
¼ teaspoon cayenne pepper

110 g packed torn kale leaves (stems and ribs removed and leaves torn into palm-size pieces)
coarse sea salt and freshly ground black pepper, to taste

1. In a large bowl, whisk together the tahini, lemon juice, olive oil, sesame seeds, garlic powder, and cayenne until smooth. Add the kale leaves, season with salt and black pepper, and toss in the dressing until completely coated. Transfer the kale leaves to a cake pan. 2. Place the pan in the air fryer and roast at 180ºC, stirring every 5 minutes, until the kale is wilted and the top is lightly browned, about 15 minutes. Remove the pan from the air fryer and serve warm.

Zesty Fried Asparagus

Prep time: 3 minutes | Cook time: 10 minutes | Serves 4

Oil, for spraying
10 to 12 spears asparagus, trimmed
2 tablespoons olive oil

1 tablespoon garlic powder
1 teaspoon chili powder
½ teaspoon ground cumin
¼ teaspoon salt

1. Line the air fryer basket with parchment and spray lightly with oil. 2. If the asparagus are too long to fit easily in the air fryer, cut them in half. 3. Place the asparagus, olive oil, garlic, chili powder, cumin, and salt in a zip-top plastic bag, seal, and toss until evenly coated. 4. Place the asparagus in the prepared basket. 5. Roast at 200ºC for 5 minutes, flip, and cook for another 5 minutes, or until bright green and firm but tender.

Glazed Carrots

Prep time: 10 minutes | Cook time: 8 to 10 minutes | Serves 4

2 teaspoons honey
1 teaspoon orange juice
½ teaspoon grated orange rind
⅛ teaspoon ginger

450 g baby carrots
2 teaspoons olive oil
¼ teaspoon salt

1. Combine honey, orange juice, grated rind, and ginger in a small bowl and set aside. 2. Toss the carrots, oil, and salt together to coat well and pour them into the air fryer basket. 3. Roast at 200ºC for 5 minutes. Shake basket to stir a little and cook for 2 to 4 minutes more, until carrots are barely tender. 4. Pour carrots into a baking pan. 5. Stir the honey mixture to combine well, pour glaze over carrots, and stir to coat. 6. Roast at 180ºC for 1 minute or just until heated through.

Parsnip Fries with Romesco Sauce

Prep time: 20 minutes | Cook time: 24 minutes | Serves 4

Romesco Sauce:
1 red pepper, halved and seeded
1 (1-inch) thick slice of Italian bread, torn into pieces
130 g almonds, toasted
Olive oil
½ Jalapeño pepper, seeded
1 tablespoon fresh parsley leaves
1 clove garlic
2 plum tomatoes, peeled and

seeded
1 tablespoon red wine vinegar
¼ teaspoon smoked paprika
½ teaspoon salt
180 ml olive oil
3 parsnips, peeled and cut into long strips
2 teaspoons olive oil
Salt and freshly ground black pepper, to taste

1. Preheat the air fryer to 200ºC. 2. Place the red pepper halves, cut side down, in the air fryer basket and air fry for 8 to 10 minutes, or until the skin turns black all over. Remove the pepper from the air fryer and let it cool. When it is cool enough to handle, peel the pepper. 3. Toss the torn bread and almonds with a little olive oil and air fry for 4 minutes, shaking the basket a couple times throughout the cooking time. When the bread and almonds are nicely toasted, remove them from the air fryer and let them cool for just a minute or two. 4. Combine the toasted bread, almonds, roasted red pepper, Jalapeño pepper, parsley, garlic, tomatoes, vinegar, smoked paprika and salt in a food processor or blender. Process until smooth. With the processor running, add the olive oil through the feed tube until the sauce comes together in a smooth paste that is barely pourable. 5. Toss the parsnip strips with the olive oil, salt and freshly ground black pepper and air fry at 200ºC for 10 minutes, shaking the basket a couple times during the cooking process so they brown and cook evenly. Serve the parsnip fries warm with the Romesco sauce to dip into.

Garlic Courgette and Red Peppers

Prep time: 5 minutes | Cook time: 15 minutes | Serves 6

2 medium courgette, cubed
1 red pepper, diced
2 garlic cloves, sliced

2 tablespoons olive oil
½ teaspoon salt

1. Preheat the air fryer to 193ºC. 2. In a large bowl, mix together the courgette, bell pepper, and garlic with the olive oil and salt. 3. Pour the mixture into the air fryer basket, and roast for 7 minutes. Shake or stir, then roast for 7 to 8 minutes more.

Easy Greek Briami (Ratatouille)

Prep time: 15 minutes | Cook time: 40 minutes | Serves 6

2 Maris Piper potatoes, cubed
100 g plum tomatoes, cubed
1 aubergine, cubed
1 courgette, cubed
1 red onion, chopped
1 red pepper, chopped
2 garlic cloves, minced
1 teaspoon dried mint
1 teaspoon dried parsley

1 teaspoon dried oregano
½ teaspoon salt
½ teaspoon black pepper
¼ teaspoon red pepper flakes
80 ml olive oil
1 (230 g) can tomato paste
65 ml vegetable stock
65 ml water

1. Preheat the air fryer to 160ºC. 2. In a large bowl, combine the potatoes, tomatoes, aubergine, courgette onion, bell pepper, garlic, mint, parsley, oregano, salt, black pepper, and red pepper flakes. 3. In a small bowl, mix together the olive oil, tomato paste, stock, and water. 4. Pour the oil-and-tomato-paste mixture over the vegetables and toss until everything is coated. 5. Pour the coated vegetables into the air fryer basket in an even layer and roast for 20 minutes. After 20 minutes, stir well and spread out again. Roast for an additional 10 minutes, then repeat the process and cook for another 10 minutes.

Mushrooms with Goat Cheese

Prep time: 10 minutes | Cook time: 10 minutes | Serves 4

3 tablespoons vegetable oil
450 g mixed mushrooms, trimmed and sliced
1 clove garlic, minced
¼ teaspoon dried thyme

½ teaspoon black pepper
110 g goat cheese, diced
2 teaspoons chopped fresh thyme leaves (optional)

1. In a baking pan, combine the oil, mushrooms, garlic, dried thyme, and pepper. Stir in the goat cheese. Place the pan in the air fryer basket. Set the air fryer to 200ºC for 10 minutes, stirring halfway through the cooking time. 2. Sprinkle with fresh thyme, if desired.

Garlic Roasted Broccoli

Prep time: 8 minutes | Cook time: 10 to 14 minutes | Serves 6

1 head broccoli, cut into bite-size florets
1 tablespoon avocado oil
2 teaspoons minced garlic
⅛ teaspoon red pepper flakes

Sea salt and freshly ground black pepper, to taste
1 tablespoon freshly squeezed lemon juice
½ teaspoon lemon zest

1. In a large bowl, toss together the broccoli, avocado oil, garlic, red pepper flakes, salt, and pepper. 2. Set the air fryer to 192ºC. Arrange the broccoli in a single layer in the air fryer basket, working in batches if necessary. Roast for 10 to 14 minutes, until the broccoli is lightly charred. 3. Place the florets in a medium bowl and toss with the lemon juice and lemon zest. Serve.

Crispy Lemon Artichoke Hearts

Prep time: 10 minutes | Cook time: 15 minutes | Serves 2

1 (425 g) can artichoke hearts in water, drained
1 egg
1 tablespoon water

30 g whole wheat bread crumbs
¼ teaspoon salt
¼ teaspoon paprika
½ lemon

1. Preheat the air fryer to 192ºC. 2. In a medium shallow bowl, beat together the egg and water until frothy. 3. In a separate medium shallow bowl, mix together the bread crumbs, salt, and paprika. 4. Dip each artichoke heart into the egg mixture, then into the bread crumb mixture, coating the outside with the crumbs. Place the artichokes hearts in a single layer of the air fryer basket. 5. Fry the artichoke hearts for 15 minutes. 6. Remove the artichokes from the air fryer, and squeeze fresh lemon juice over the top before serving.

Butter and Garlic Fried Cabbage

Prep time: 5 minutes | Cook time: 9 minutes | Serves 2

Oil, for spraying
½ head cabbage, cut into bite-size pieces
2 tablespoons unsalted butter, melted

1 teaspoon granulated garlic
½ teaspoon coarse sea salt
¼ teaspoon freshly ground black pepper

1. Line the air fryer basket with parchment and spray lightly with oil. 2. In a large bowl, mix together the cabbage, butter, garlic, salt, and black pepper until evenly coated. 3. Transfer the cabbage to the prepared basket and spray lightly with oil. 4. Air fry at 192ºC for 5 minutes, toss, and cook for another 3 to 4 minutes, or until lightly crispy.

Corn Croquettes

Prep time: 10 minutes | Cook time: 12 to 14 minutes | Serves 4

105 g leftover mashed potatoes
340 g corn kernels (if frozen, thawed, and well drained)
¼ teaspoon onion powder
⅛ teaspoon ground black

pepper
¼ teaspoon salt
50 g panko bread crumbs
Oil for misting or cooking spray

1. Place the potatoes and half the corn in food processor and pulse until corn is well chopped. 2. Transfer mixture to large bowl and stir in remaining corn, onion powder, pepper and salt. 3. Shape mixture into 16 balls. 4. Roll balls in panko crumbs, mist with oil or cooking spray, and place in air fryer basket. 5. Air fry at 180ºC for 12 to 14 minutes, until golden brown and crispy

Fried Courgette Salad

Prep time: 10 minutes | Cook time: 5 to 7 minutes | Serves 4

2 medium courgette, thinly sliced
5 tablespoons olive oil, divided
15 g chopped fresh parsley
2 tablespoons chopped fresh mint

Zest and juice of ½ lemon
1 clove garlic, minced
65 g crumbled feta cheese
Freshly ground black pepper, to taste

1. Preheat the air fryer to 200ºC. 2. In a large bowl, toss the courgette slices with 1 tablespoon of the olive oil. 3. Working in batches if necessary, arrange the courgette slices in an even layer in the air fryer basket. Pausing halfway through the cooking time to shake the basket, air fry for 5 to 7 minutes until soft and lightly browned on each side. 4. Meanwhile, in a small bowl, combine the remaining 4 tablespoons olive oil, parsley, mint, lemon zest, lemon juice, and garlic. 5. Arrange the courgette on a plate and drizzle with the dressing. Sprinkle the feta and black pepper on top. Serve warm or at room temperature.

Parmesan-Thyme Butternut Squash

Prep time: 15 minutes | Cook time: 20 minutes | Serves 4

350 g butternut squash, cubed into 1-inch pieces (approximately 1 medium)
2 tablespoons olive oil
¼ teaspoon salt

¼ teaspoon garlic powder
¼ teaspoon black pepper
1 tablespoon fresh thyme
20 g grated Parmesan

1. Preheat the air fryer to 180ºC. 2. In a large bowl, combine the cubed squash with the olive oil, salt, garlic powder, pepper, and thyme until the squash is well coated. 3. Pour this mixture into the air fryer basket, and roast for 10 minutes. Stir and roast another 8 to 10 minutes more. 4. Remove the squash from the air fryer and toss with freshly grated Parmesan before serving.

Tofu Bites

Prep time: 15 minutes | Cook time: 30 minutes | Serves 4

1 packaged firm tofu, cubed and pressed to remove excess water
1 tablespoon soy sauce
1 tablespoon ketchup
1 tablespoon maple syrup
½ teaspoon vinegar
1 teaspoon liquid smoke

1 teaspoon hot sauce
2 tablespoons sesame seeds
1 teaspoon garlic powder
Salt and ground black pepper, to taste
Cooking spray

1. Preheat the air fryer to 192ºC. 2. Spritz a baking dish with cooking spray. 3. Combine all the ingredients to coat the tofu completely and allow the marinade to absorb for half an hour. 4. Transfer the tofu to the baking dish, then air fry for 15 minutes. Flip the tofu over and air fry for another 15 minutes on the other side. 5. Serve immediately.

Fried Brussels Sprouts

Prep time: 10 minutes | Cook time: 18 minutes | Serves 4

1 teaspoon plus 1 tablespoon extra-virgin olive oil, divided
2 teaspoons minced garlic
2 tablespoons honey
1 tablespoon sugar
2 tablespoons freshly squeezed lemon juice
2 tablespoons rice vinegar

2 tablespoons sriracha
450 g Brussels sprouts, stems trimmed and any tough leaves removed, rinsed, halved lengthwise, and dried
½ teaspoon salt
Cooking oil spray

1. In a small saucepan over low heat, combine 1 teaspoon of olive oil, the garlic, honey, sugar, lemon juice, vinegar, and sriracha. Cook for 2 to 3 minutes, or until slightly thickened. Remove the pan from the heat, cover, and set aside. 2. Place the Brussels sprouts in a resealable bag or small bowl. Add the remaining olive oil and the salt, and toss to coat. 3. Insert the crisper plate into the basket and the basket into the unit. Preheat the unit by selecting AIR FRY, setting the temperature to 200ºC, and setting the time to 3 minutes. Select START/STOP to begin. 4. Once the unit is preheated, spray the crisper plate with cooking oil. Add the Brussels sprouts to the basket. 5. Select AIR FRY, set the temperature to 200ºC, and set the time to 15 minutes. Select START/STOP to begin. 6. After 7 or 8 minutes, remove the basket and shake it to toss the sprouts. Reinsert the basket to resume cooking. 7. When the cooking is complete, the leaves should be crispy and light brown and the sprout centres tender. 8. Place the sprouts in a medium serving bowl and drizzle the sauce over the top. Toss to coat, and serve immediately.

Sausage-Stuffed Mushroom Caps

Prep time: 10 minutes | Cook time: 8 minutes | Serves 2

6 large portobello mushroom caps	2 tablespoons blanched finely ground almond flour
230 g Italian sausage	20 g grated Parmesan cheese
15 g chopped onion	1 teaspoon minced fresh garlic

1. Use a spoon to hollow out each mushroom cap, reserving scrapings. 2. In a medium skillet over medium heat, brown the sausage about 10 minutes or until fully cooked and no pink remains. Drain and then add reserved mushroom scrapings, onion, almond flour, Parmesan, and garlic. Gently fold ingredients together and continue cooking an additional minute, then remove from heat. 3. Evenly spoon the mixture into mushroom caps and place the caps into a 6-inch round pan. Place pan into the air fryer basket. 4. Adjust the temperature to 192°C and set the timer for 8 minutes. 5. When finished cooking, the tops will be browned and bubbling. Serve warm.

Lush Vegetable Salad

Prep time: 15 minutes | Cook time: 10 minutes | Serves 4

6 plum tomatoes, halved	oil
2 large red onions, sliced	1 teaspoon paprika
4 long red pepper, sliced	½ lemon, juiced
2 yellow pepper, sliced	Salt and ground black pepper, to taste
6 cloves garlic, crushed	
1 tablespoon extra-virgin olive	1 tablespoon baby capers

1. Preheat the air fryer to 220°C. 2. Put the tomatoes, onions, peppers, and garlic in a large bowl and cover with the extra-virgin olive oil, paprika, and lemon juice. Sprinkle with salt and pepper as desired. 3. Line the inside of the air fryer basket with aluminum foil. Put the vegetables inside and air fry for 10 minutes, ensuring the edges turn brown. 4. Serve in a salad bowl with the baby capers.

Burger Bun for One

Prep time: 2 minutes | Cook time: 5 minutes | Serves 1

2 tablespoons salted butter, melted	¼ teaspoon baking powder
	⅛ teaspoon apple cider vinegar
25 g blanched finely ground almond flour	1 large egg, whisked

1. Pour butter into an ungreased ramekin. Add flour, baking powder, and vinegar to ramekin and stir until combined. Add egg and stir until batter is mostly smooth. 2. Place ramekin into air fryer basket. Adjust the temperature to 180°C and bake for 5 minutes. When done, the centre will be firm and the top slightly browned. Let cool, about 5 minutes, then remove from ramekin and slice in half. Serve.

Spiced Butternut Squash

Prep time: 10 minutes | Cook time: 15 minutes | Serves 4

600 g 1-inch-cubed butternut squash	1 to 2 tablespoons brown sugar
2 tablespoons vegetable oil	1 teaspoon Chinese five-spice powder

1. In a medium bowl, combine the squash, oil, sugar, and five-spice powder. Toss to coat. 2. Place the squash in the air fryer basket. Set the air fryer to 200°C for 15 minutes or until tender.

Baked Jalapeño and Cheese Cauliflower Mash

Prep time: 10 minutes | Cook time: 15 minutes | Serves 6

1 (340 g) steamer bag cauliflower florets, cooked according to package instructions	120 g shredded sharp Cheddar cheese
	20 g pickled jalapeños
	½ teaspoon salt
2 tablespoons salted butter, softened	¼ teaspoon ground black pepper
60 g cream cheese, softened	

1. Place cooked cauliflower into a food processor with remaining ingredients. Pulse twenty times until cauliflower is smooth and all ingredients are combined. 2. Spoon mash into an ungreased round nonstick baking dish. Place dish into air fryer basket. Adjust the temperature to 192°C and bake for 15 minutes. The top will be golden brown when done. Serve warm.

Flatbread

Prep time: 5 minutes | Cook time: 7 minutes | Serves 2

225 g shredded Mozzarella cheese
25 g blanched finely ground almond flour
30 g full-fat cream cheese, softened

1. In a large microwave-safe bowl, melt Mozzarella in the microwave for 30 seconds. Stir in almond flour until smooth and then add cream cheese. Continue mixing until dough forms, gently kneading it with wet hands if necessary. 2. Divide the dough into two pieces and roll out to ¼-inch thickness between two pieces of parchment. Cut another piece of parchment to fit your air fryer basket. 3. Place a piece of flatbread onto your parchment and into the air fryer, working in two batches if needed. 4. Adjust the temperature to 160°C and air fry for 7 minutes. 5. Halfway through the cooking time flip the flatbread. Serve warm.

Broccoli with Sesame Dressing

Prep time: 5 minutes | Cook time: 10 minutes | Serves 4

425 g broccoli florets, cut into
bite-size pieces
1 tablespoon olive oil
¼ teaspoon salt
2 tablespoons sesame seeds
2 tablespoons rice vinegar

2 tablespoons coconut aminos
2 tablespoons sesame oil
½ teaspoon xylitol
¼ teaspoon red pepper flakes
(optional)

1. Preheat the air fryer to 200ºC. 2. In a large bowl, toss the broccoli with the olive oil and salt until thoroughly coated. 3. Transfer the broccoli to the air fryer basket. Pausing halfway through the cooking time to shake the basket, air fry for 10 minutes until the stems are tender and the edges are beginning to crisp. 4. Meanwhile, in the same large bowl, whisk together the sesame seeds, vinegar, coconut aminos, sesame oil, xylitol, and red pepper flakes (if using). 5. Transfer the broccoli to the bowl and toss until thoroughly coated with the seasonings. Serve warm or at room temperature.

Crispy Chickpeas

Prep time: 5 minutes | Cook time: 15 minutes | Serves 4

1 (425 g) can chickpeas,
drained but not rinsed
2 tablespoons olive oil

1 teaspoon salt
2 tablespoons lemon juice

1. Preheat the air fryer to 200ºC. 2. Add all the ingredients together in a bowl and mix. Transfer this mixture to the air fryer basket. 3. Air fry for 15 minutes, ensuring the chickpeas become nice and crispy. 4. Serve immediately.

Breaded Green Tomatoes

Prep time: 15 minutes | Cook time: 30 minutes | Serves 4

60 g plain flour
2 eggs
60 g semolina
60 g panko bread crumbs
1 teaspoon garlic powder

Salt and freshly ground black
pepper, to taste
2 green tomatoes, cut into
½-inch-thick rounds
Cooking oil spray

1. Place the flour in a small bowl. 2. In another small bowl, beat the eggs. 3. In a third small bowl, stir together the semolina, panko, and garlic powder. Season with salt and pepper. 4. Dip each tomato slice into the flour, the egg, and finally the semolina mixture to coat. 5. Insert the crisper plate into the basket and the basket into the unit. Preheat the unit by selecting AIR FRY, setting the temperature to 200ºC, and setting the time to 3 minutes. Select START/STOP to begin. 6. Once the unit is preheated, spray the crisper plate and the basket with cooking oil. Working in batches,

place the tomato slices in the air fryer in a single layer. Do not stack them. Spray the tomato slices with the cooking oil. 7. Select AIR FRY, set the temperature to 200ºC, and set the time to 10 minutes. Select START/STOP to begin. 8. After 5 minutes, use tongs to flip the tomatoes. Resume cooking for 4 to 5 minutes, or until crisp. 9. When the cooking is complete, transfer the fried green tomatoes to a plate. Repeat steps 6, 7, and 8 for the remaining tomatoes.

Parmesan Mushrooms

Prep time: 5 minutes | Cook time: 15 minutes | Serves 4

Oil, for spraying
450 g shitake mushrooms,
stems trimmed
2 tablespoons olive oil
2 teaspoons granulated garlic
1 teaspoon onion powder

½ teaspoon salt
¼ teaspoon freshly ground
black pepper
30 g grated Parmesan cheese,
divided

1. Line the air fryer basket with parchment and spray lightly with oil. 2. In a large bowl, toss the mushrooms with the olive oil, garlic, onion powder, salt, and black pepper until evenly coated. 3. Place the mushrooms in the prepared basket. 4. Roast at 192ºC for 13 minutes. 5. Sprinkle half of the cheese over the mushrooms and cook for another 2 minutes. 6. Transfer the mushrooms to a serving bowl, add the remaining Parmesan cheese, and toss until evenly coated. Serve immediately.

Courgette Balls

Prep time: 5 minutes | Cook time: 10 minutes | Serves 4

4 courgettes
1 egg
45 g grated Parmesan cheese

1 tablespoon Italian herbs
75 g grated coconut

1. Thinly grate the courgettes and dry with a cheesecloth, ensuring to remove all the moisture. 2. In a bowl, combine the courgettes with the egg, Parmesan, Italian herbs, and grated coconut, mixing well to incorporate everything. Using the hands, mold the mixture into balls. 3. Preheat the air fryer to 200ºC. 4. Lay the courgette balls in the air fryer basket and air fry for 10 minutes. 5. Serve hot.

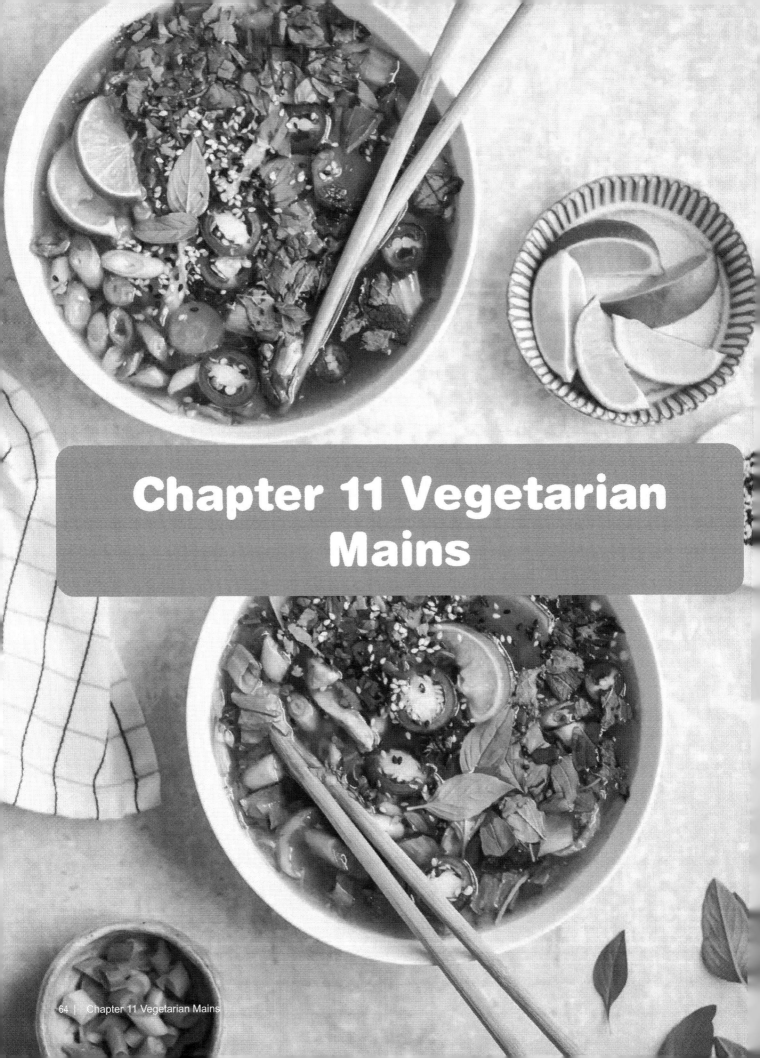

Chapter 11 Vegetarian Mains

Chapter 11 Vegetarian Mains

Broccoli Crust Pizza

Prep time: 15 minutes | Cook time: 12 minutes | Serves 4

700 ml riced broccoli, steamed and drained well

1 large egg

120 ml grated vegetarian Parmesan cheese

3 tablespoons low-carb Alfredo sauce

120 ml shredded Mozzarella cheese

In a large bowl, mix broccoli, egg, and Parmesan. Cut a piece of parchment to fit your air fryer basket. Press out the pizza mixture to fit on the parchment, working in two batches if necessary. Place into the air fryer basket. Adjust the temperature to 188ºC and air fry for 5 minutes. The crust should be firm enough to flip. If not, add 2 additional minutes. Flip crust. Top with Alfredo sauce and Mozzarella. Return to the air fryer basket and cook an additional 7 minutes or until cheese is golden and bubbling. Serve warm.

Garlicky Sesame Carrots

Prep time: 5 minutes | Cook time: 16 minutes | Serves 4 to 6

450 g baby carrots	Freshly ground black pepper, to
1 tablespoon sesame oil	taste
½ teaspoon dried dill	6 cloves garlic, peeled
Pinch salt	3 tablespoons sesame seeds

Preheat the air fryer to 192ºC. In a medium bowl, drizzle the baby carrots with the sesame oil. Sprinkle with the dill, salt, and pepper and toss to coat well. Place the baby carrots in the air fryer basket and roast for 8 minutes. Remove the basket and stir in the garlic. Return the basket to the air fryer and roast for another 8 minutes, or until the carrots are lightly browned. Serve sprinkled with the sesame seeds.

Cheese Stuffed Peppers

Prep time: 20 minutes | Cook time: 15 minutes | Serves 2

1 red pepper, top and seeds removed	Salt and pepper, to taste
	235 ml Cottage cheese
1 yellow pepper, top and seeds removed	4 tablespoons mayonnaise
	2 pickles, chopped

Arrange the peppers in the lightly greased air fryer basket. Cook in the preheated air fryer at 204ºC for 15 minutes, turning them over halfway through the cooking time. Season with salt and pepper. Then, in a mixing bowl, combine the soft white cheese with the mayonnaise and chopped pickles. Stuff the pepper with the soft white cheese mixture and serve. Enjoy!

Black Bean and Tomato Chilli

Prep time: 15 minutes | Cook time: 23 minutes | Serves 6

1 tablespoon olive oil	2 cans diced tomatoes
1 medium onion, diced	2 chipotle peppers, chopped
3 garlic cloves, minced	2 teaspoons cumin
235 ml vegetable broth	2 teaspoons chilli powder
3 cans black beans, drained and rinsed	1 teaspoon dried oregano
	½ teaspoon salt

Over a medium heat, fry the garlic and onions in the olive oil for 3 minutes. Add the remaining ingredients, stirring constantly and scraping the bottom to prevent sticking. Preheat the air fryer to 204ºC. Take a dish and place the mixture inside. Put a sheet of aluminium foil on top. Transfer to the air fryer and bake for 20 minutes. When ready, plate up and serve immediately.

Tangy Asparagus and Broccoli

Prep time: 25 minutes | Cook time: 22 minutes | Serves 4

230 g asparagus, cut into 1½-inch pieces	Salt and white pepper, to taste
	120 ml vegetable broth
230 g broccoli, cut into 1½-inch pieces	2 tablespoons apple cider vinegar
2 tablespoons olive oil	

Place the vegetables in a single layer in the lightly greased air fryer basket. Drizzle the olive oil over the vegetables. Sprinkle with salt and white pepper. Cook at 192ºC for 15 minutes, shaking the basket halfway through the cooking time. Add 120 ml of vegetable broth to a saucepan; bring to a rapid boil and add the vinegar. Cook for 5 to 7 minutes or until the sauce has reduced by half. Spoon the sauce over the warm vegetables and serve immediately. Bon appétit!

Potato and Broccoli with Tofu Scramble

Prep time: 15 minutes | Cook time: 30 minutes | Serves 3

600 ml chopped red potato

2 tablespoons olive oil, divided

1 block tofu, chopped finely

2 tablespoons tamari

1 teaspoon turmeric powder

½ teaspoon onion powder

½ teaspoon garlic powder

120 ml chopped onion

1 L broccoli florets

Preheat the air fryer to 204ºC. Toss together the potatoes and 1 tablespoon of the olive oil. Air fry the potatoes in a baking dish for 15 minutes, shaking once during the cooking time to ensure they fry evenly. Combine the tofu, the remaining 1 tablespoon of the olive oil, turmeric, onion powder, tamari, and garlic powder together, stirring in the onions, followed by the broccoli. Top the potatoes with the tofu mixture and air fry for an additional 15 minutes. Serve warm.

Aubergine and Courgette Bites

Prep time: 30 minutes | Cook time: 30 minutes | Serves 8

2 teaspoons fresh mint leaves, chopped

1½ teaspoons red pepper chilli flakes

2 tablespoons melted butter

450 g aubergine, peeled and cubed

450 g courgette, peeled and cubed

3 tablespoons olive oil

Toss all the above ingredients in a large-sized mixing dish. Roast the aubergine and courgette bites for 30 minutes at 164ºC in your air fryer, turning once or twice. Serve with a homemade dipping sauce.

Spaghetti Squash Alfredo

Prep time: 10 minutes | Cook time: 15 minutes | Serves 2

½ large cooked spaghetti squash

2 tablespoons salted butter, melted

120 ml low-carb Alfredo sauce

60 ml grated vegetarian Parmesan cheese

½ teaspoon garlic powder

1 teaspoon dried parsley

¼ teaspoon ground peppercorn

120 ml shredded Italian blend cheese

Using a fork, remove the strands of spaghetti squash from the shell. Place into a large bowl with butter and Alfredo sauce. Sprinkle with Parmesan, garlic powder, parsley, and peppercorn. Pour into a 1 L round baking dish and top with shredded cheese. Place dish into the air fryer basket. Adjust the temperature to 160ºC and bake for 15 minutes. When finished, cheese will be golden and bubbling. Serve immediately.

Mediterranean Pan Pizza

Prep time: 5 minutes | Cook time: 8 minutes | Serves 2

235 ml shredded Mozzarella cheese

¼ medium red pepper, seeded and chopped

120 ml chopped fresh spinach

leaves

2 tablespoons chopped black olives

2 tablespoons crumbled feta cheese

Sprinkle Mozzarella into an ungreased round non-stick baking dish in an even layer. Add remaining ingredients on top. Place dish into air fryer basket. Adjust the temperature to 176ºC and bake for 8 minutes, checking halfway through to avoid burning. Top of pizza will be golden brown, and the cheese melted when done. Remove dish from fryer and let cool 5 minutes before slicing and serving.

White Cheddar and Mushroom Soufflés

Prep time: 15 minutes | Cook time: 12 minutes | Serves 4

3 large eggs, whites and yolks separated

120 ml extra mature white Cheddar cheese

85 g soft white cheese

¼ teaspoon cream of tartar

¼ teaspoon salt

¼ teaspoon ground black pepper

120 ml chestnut mushrooms, sliced

In a large bowl, whip egg whites until stiff peaks form, about 2 minutes. In a separate large bowl, beat Cheddar, egg yolks, soft white cheese, cream of tartar, salt, and pepper together until combined. Fold egg whites into cheese mixture, being careful not to stir. Fold in mushrooms, then pour mixture evenly into four ungreased ramekins. Place ramekins into air fryer basket. Adjust the temperature to 176ºC and bake for 12 minutes. Eggs will be browned on the top and firm in the centre when done. Serve warm.

Mushroom and Pepper Pizza Squares

Prep time: 10 minutes | Cook time: 10 minutes | Serves 10

1 pizza dough, cut into squares

235 ml chopped oyster mushrooms

1 shallot, chopped

¼ red pepper, chopped

2 tablespoons parsley

Salt and ground black pepper, to taste

Preheat the air fryer to 204ºC. In a bowl, combine the oyster mushrooms, shallot, pepper and parsley. Sprinkle some salt and pepper as desired. Spread this mixture on top of the pizza squares. Bake in the air fryer for 10 minutes. Serve warm.

Rosemary Beetroots with Balsamic Glaze

Prep time: 5 minutes | Cook time: 10 minutes | Serves 2

Beetroot:	Salt and black pepper, to taste
2 beetroots, cubed	Balsamic Glaze:
2 tablespoons olive oil	80 ml balsamic vinegar
2 sprigs rosemary, chopped	1 tablespoon honey

Preheat the air fryer to 204ºC. Combine the beetroots, olive oil, rosemary, salt, and pepper in a mixing bowl and toss until the beetroots are completely coated. Place the beetroots in the air fryer basket and air fry for 10 minutes until the beetroots are crisp and browned at the edges. Shake the basket halfway through the cooking time. Meanwhile, make the balsamic glaze: Place the balsamic vinegar and honey in a small saucepan and bring to a boil over medium heat. When the sauce starts to boil, reduce the heat to medium-low heat and simmer until the liquid is reduced by half. When ready, remove the beetroots from the basket to a platter. Pour the balsamic glaze over the top and serve immediately.

Almond-Cauliflower Gnocchi

Prep time: 5 minutes | Cook time: 25 to 30 minutes | Serves 4

1.2 L cauliflower florets	60 ml unsalted butter, melted
160 ml almond flour	60 ml grated Parmesan cheese
½ teaspoon salt	

In a food processor fitted with a metal blade, pulse the cauliflower until finely chopped. Transfer the cauliflower to a large microwave-safe bowl and cover it with a paper towel. Microwave for 5 minutes. Spread the cauliflower on a towel to cool. When cool enough to handle, draw up the sides of the towel and squeeze tightly over a sink to remove the excess moisture. Return the cauliflower to the food processor and whirl until creamy. Sprinkle in the flour and salt and pulse until a sticky dough comes together. Transfer the dough to a workspace lightly floured with almond flour. Shape the dough into a ball and divide into 4 equal sections. Roll each section into a rope 1 inch thick. Slice the dough into squares with a sharp knife. Preheat the air fryer to 204ºC. Working in batches if necessary, place the gnocchi in a single layer in the basket of the air fryer and spray generously with olive oil. Pausing halfway through the cooking time to turn the gnocchi, air fry for 25 to 30 minutes until golden brown and crispy on the edges. Transfer to a large bowl and toss with the melted butter and Parmesan cheese.

Crustless Spinach Cheese Pie

Prep time: 10 minutes | Cook time: 20 minutes | Serves 4

6 large eggs	235 ml shredded sharp Cheddar cheese
60 ml double cream	60 ml diced brown onion
235 ml frozen chopped spinach, drained	

In a medium bowl, whisk eggs and add cream. Add remaining ingredients to bowl. Pour into a round baking dish. Place into the air fryer basket. Adjust the temperature to 160ºC and bake for 20 minutes. Eggs will be firm and slightly browned when cooked. Serve immediately.

Crispy Tofu

Prep time: 30 minutes | Cook time: 15 to 20 minutes | Serves 4

1 (454 g) block extra-firm tofu	1 tablespoon chilli-garlic sauce
2 tablespoons coconut aminos	1½ teaspoons black sesame seeds
1 tablespoon toasted sesame oil	1 spring onion, thinly sliced
1 tablespoon olive oil	

Press the tofu for at least 15 minutes by wrapping it in paper towels and setting a heavy pan on top so that the moisture drains. Slice the tofu into bite-size cubes and transfer to a bowl. Drizzle with the coconut aminos, sesame oil, olive oil, and chilli-garlic sauce. Cover and refrigerate for 1 hour or up to overnight. Preheat the air fryer to 204ºC. Arrange the tofu in a single layer in the air fryer basket. Pausing to shake the pan halfway through the cooking time, air fry for 15 to 20 minutes until crisp. Serve with any juices that accumulate in the bottom of the air fryer, sprinkled with the sesame seeds and sliced spring onion.

Chapter 12 Desserts

Chapter 12 Desserts

Caramelized Fruit Skewers

Prep time: 10 minutes | Cook time: 3 to 5 minutes | Serves 4

2 peaches, peeled, pitted, and thickly sliced
3 plums, halved and pitted
3 nectarines, halved and pitted
1 tablespoon honey

½ teaspoon ground cinnamon
¼ teaspoon ground allspice
Pinch cayenne pepper
Special Equipment:
8 metal skewers

1. Preheat the air fryer to 204°C. 2. Thread, alternating peaches, plums, and nectarines, onto the metal skewers that fit into the air fryer. 3. Thoroughly combine the honey, cinnamon, allspice, and cayenne in a small bowl. Brush the glaze generously over the fruit skewers. 4. Transfer the fruit skewers to the air fryer basket. You may need to cook in batches to avoid overcrowding. 5. Air fry for 3 to 5 minutes, or until the fruit is caramelized. 6. Remove from the basket and repeat with the remaining fruit skewers. 7. Let the fruit skewers rest for 5 minutes before serving.

Cream Cheese Danish

Prep time: 20 minutes | Cook time: 15 minutes | Serves 6

70 g blanched finely ground almond flour
225 g shredded Mozzarella cheese
140 g full-fat cream cheese, divided

2 large egg yolks
75 g powdered sweetener, divided
2 teaspoons vanilla extract, divided

1. In a large microwave-safe bowl, add almond flour, Mozzarella, and 30 g cream cheese. Mix and then microwave for 1 minute. 2. Stir and add egg yolks to the bowl. Continue stirring until soft dough forms. Add 50 g sweetener to dough and 1 teaspoon vanilla. 3. Cut a piece of baking paper to fit your air fryer basket. Wet your hands with warm water and press out the dough into a ¼-inch-thick rectangle. 4. In a medium bowl, mix remaining cream cheese, remaining sweetener, and vanilla. Place this cream cheese mixture on the right half of the dough rectangle. Fold over the left side of the dough and press to seal. Place into the air fryer basket. 5. Adjust the temperature to 164°C and bake for 15 minutes. 6. After 7 minutes, flip over the Danish. 7. When done, remove the Danish from baking paper and allow to completely cool before cutting.

Coconut Flour Cake

Prep time: 10 minutes | Cook time: 25 minutes | Serves 6

2 tablespoons salted butter, melted
35 g coconut flour
2 large eggs, whisked

100 g granulated sweetener
1 teaspoon baking powder
1 teaspoon vanilla extract
120 ml sour cream

1. Mix all ingredients in a large bowl. Pour batter into an ungreased round nonstick baking dish. 2. Place baking dish into air fryer basket. Adjust the temperature to 148°C and bake for 25 minutes. The cake will be dark golden on top, and a toothpick inserted in the center should come out clean when done. 3. Let cool in dish 15 minutes before slicing and serving.

Spiced Apple Cake

Prep time: 15 minutes | Cook time: 30 minutes | Serves 6

Vegetable oil
2 diced & peeled Gala apples
1 tablespoon fresh lemon juice
55 g unsalted butter, softened
65 g granulated sugar
2 large eggs
155 g plain flour
1½ teaspoons baking powder

1 tablespoon apple pie spice
½ teaspoon ground ginger
¼ teaspoon ground cardamom
¼ teaspoon ground nutmeg
½ teaspoon kosher, or coarse sea salt
60 ml whole milk
Icing sugar, for dusting

1. Grease a 0.7-liter Bundt, or tube pan with oil; set aside. 2. In a medium bowl, toss the apples with the lemon juice until well coated; set aside. 3. In a large bowl, combine the butter and sugar. Beat with an electric hand mixer on medium speed until the sugar has dissolved. Add the eggs and beat until fluffy. Add the flour, baking powder, apple pie spice, ginger, cardamom, nutmeg, salt, and milk. Mix until the batter is thick but pourable. 4. Pour the batter into the prepared pan. Top batter evenly with the apple mixture. Place the pan in the air fryer basket. Set the air fryer to 176°C and cook for 30 minutes, or until a toothpick inserted in the center of the cake comes out clean. Close the air fryer and let the cake rest for 10 minutes. Turn the cake out onto a wire rack and cool completely. 5. Right before serving, dust the cake with icing sugar.

Baked Brazilian Pineapple

Prep time: 10 minutes | Cook time: 10 minutes | Serves 4

95 g brown sugar
2 teaspoons ground cinnamon
1 small pineapple, peeled,

cored, and cut into spears
3 tablespoons unsalted butter, melted

1. In a small bowl, mix the brown sugar and cinnamon until thoroughly combined. 2. Brush the pineapple spears with the melted butter. Sprinkle the cinnamon-sugar over the spears, pressing lightly to ensure it adheres well. 3. Place the spears in the air fryer basket in a single layer. (Depending on the size of your air fryer, you may have to do this in batches.) Set the air fryer to 204°C and cook for 10 minutes for the first batch (6 to 8 minutes for the next batch, as the fryer will be preheated). Halfway through the cooking time, brush the spears with butter. 4. The pineapple spears are done when they are heated through, and the sugar is bubbling. Serve hot.

Apple Dutch Baby

Prep time: 30 minutes | Cook time: 16 minutes | Serves 2 to 3

Batter:
2 large eggs
30 g plain flour
¼ teaspoon baking powder
1½ teaspoons granulated sugar
Pinch kosher, or coarse sea salt
120 ml whole milk
1 tablespoon butter, melted
½ teaspoon pure vanilla extract
¼ teaspoon ground nutmeg

Apples:
2 tablespoon butter
4 tablespoons granulated sugar
¼ teaspoon ground cinnamon
¼ teaspoon ground nutmeg
1 small tart apple (such as Granny Smith), peeled, cored, and sliced
Vanilla ice cream (optional), for serving

1. For the batter: In a medium bowl, combine the eggs, flour, baking powder, sugar, and salt. Whisk lightly. While whisking continuously, slowly pour in the milk. Whisk in the melted butter, vanilla, and nutmeg. Let the batter stand for 30 minutes. (You can also cover and refrigerate overnight.) 2. For the apples: Place the butter in a baking pan. Place the pan in the air fryer basket. Set the air fryer to 204°C and cook for 2 minutes. In a small bowl, combine 2 tablespoons of the sugar with the cinnamon and nutmeg and stir until well combined. 3. When the pan is hot and the butter is melted, brush some butter up the sides of the pan. Sprinkle the spiced sugar mixture over the butter. Arrange the apple slices in the pan in a single layer and sprinkle the remaining 2 tablespoons sugar over the apples. Keep the air fryer at 204°C and cook for a further2 minutes, or until the mixture bubbles. 4. Gently pour the batter over the apples. Set the air fryer to 176°C cooking for 12 minutes, or until the pancake is golden brown around the edges, the center is cooked through, and a toothpick emerges clean. 5. Serve immediately with ice cream, if desired.

Chocolate Soufflés

Prep time: 5 minutes | Cook time: 14 minutes | Serves 2

Butter and sugar for greasing the ramekins
85 g semi-sweet chocolate, chopped
55 g unsalted butter
2 eggs, yolks and white separated

3 tablespoons granulated sugar
½ teaspoon pure vanilla extract
2 tablespoons plain flour
Icing sugar, for dusting the finished soufflés
Heavy cream, for serving

1. Butter and sugar two 6-ounce (170 g) ramekins. (Butter the ramekins and then coat the butter with sugar by shaking it around in the ramekin and dumping out any excess.) 2. Melt the chocolate and butter together, either in the microwave or in a double boiler. In a separate bowl, beat the egg yolks vigorously. Add the sugar and the vanilla extract and beat well again. Drizzle in the chocolate and butter, mixing well. Stir in the flour, combining until there are no lumps. 3. Preheat the air fryer to 164°C. 4. In a separate bowl, whisk the egg whites to soft peak stage (the point at which the whites can almost stand up on the end of your whisk). Fold the whipped egg whites into the chocolate mixture gently and in stages. 5. Transfer the batter carefully to the buttered ramekins, leaving about ½-inch at the top. (You may have a little extra batter, depending on how airy the batter is, so you might be able to squeeze out a third soufflé if you want to.) Place the ramekins into the air fryer basket and air fry for 14 minutes. The soufflés should have risen nicely and be brown on top. (Don't worry if the top gets a little dark, you'll be covering it with icing sugar in the next step.) 6. Dust with icing sugar and serve immediately with heavy cream to pour over the top at the table.

Fried Oreos

Prep time: 7 minutes | Cook time: 6 minutes per batch | Makes 12 cookies

Coconut, or avocado oil for misting, or nonstick spray
120 g ready-made pancake mix
1 teaspoon vanilla extract
120 ml water, plus 2

tablespoons
12 Oreos or other chocolate sandwich biscuits
1 tablespoon icing sugar

1. Spray baking pan with oil or nonstick spray and place in basket. 2. Preheat the air fryer to 200°C. 3. In a medium bowl, mix together the pancake mix, vanilla, and water. 4. Dip 4 cookies in batter and place in baking pan. 5. Cook for 6 minutes, until browned. 6. Repeat steps 4 and 5 for the remaining cookies. 7. Sift icing sugar over warm cookies.

Berry Crumble

Prep time: 10 minutes | Cook time: 15 minutes | Serves 4

For the Filling:	20 g rolled oats
300 g mixed berries	1 tablespoon granulated sugar
2 tablespoons sugar	2 tablespoons cold unsalted
1 tablespoon cornflour	butter, cut into small cubes
1 tablespoon fresh lemon juice	Whipped cream or ice cream
For the Topping:	(optional)
30 g plain flour	

1. Preheat the air fryer to 204ºC. 2. For the filling: In a round baking pan, gently mix the berries, sugar, cornflour, and lemon juice until thoroughly combined. 3. For the topping: In a small bowl, combine the flour, oats, and sugar. Stir the butter into the flour mixture until the mixture has the consistency of breadcrumbs. 4. Sprinkle the topping over the berries. 5. Put the pan in the air fryer basket and air fry for 15 minutes. Let cool for 5 minutes on a wire rack. 6. Serve topped with whipped cream or ice cream, if desired.

Gingerbread

Prep time: 5 minutes | Cook time: 20 minutes |
Makes 1 loaf

Cooking spray	⅛ teaspoon salt
125 g plain flour	1 egg
2 tablespoons granulated sugar	70 g treacle
¾ teaspoon ground ginger	120 ml buttermilk
¼ teaspoon cinnamon	2 tablespoons coconut, or
1 teaspoon baking powder	avocado oil
½ teaspoon baking soda	1 teaspoon pure vanilla extract

1. Preheat the air fryer to 164ºC. 2. Spray a baking dish lightly with cooking spray. 3. In a medium bowl, mix together all the dry ingredients. 4. In a separate bowl, beat the egg. Add treacle, buttermilk, oil, and vanilla and stir until well mixed. 5. Pour liquid mixture into dry ingredients and stir until well blended. 6. Pour batter into baking dish and bake for 20 minutes, or until toothpick inserted in center of loaf comes out clean.

Chocolate Bread Pudding

Prep time: 10 minutes | Cook time: 10 to 12 minutes | Serves 4

Nonstick, flour-infused baking	2 tablespoons cocoa powder
spray	3 tablespoons light brown sugar
1 egg	3 tablespoons peanut butter
1 egg yolk	1 teaspoon vanilla extract
175 ml chocolate milk	5 slices firm white bread, cubed

1. Spray a 6-by-2-inch round baking pan with the baking spray.

Set aside. 2. In a medium bowl, whisk the egg, egg yolk, chocolate milk, cocoa powder, brown sugar, peanut butter, and vanilla until thoroughly combined. Stir in the bread cubes and let soak for 10 minutes. Spoon this mixture into the prepared pan. 3. Insert the crisper plate into the basket and the basket into the unit. Preheat the unit to 164ºC. 4. cook the pudding for about 10 minutes and then check if done. It is done when it is firm to the touch. If not, resume cooking. 5. When the cooking is complete, let the pudding cool for 5 minutes. Serve warm.

Oatmeal Raisin Bars

Prep time: 15 minutes | Cook time: 15 minutes | Serves 8

40 g plain flour	50 g granulated sugar
¼ teaspoon kosher, or coarse	120 ml canola, or rapeseed oil
sea salt	1 large egg
¼ teaspoon baking powder	1 teaspoon vanilla extract
¼ teaspoon ground cinnamon	110 g quick-cooking oats
50 g light brown sugar, lightly	60 g raisins
packed	

1. Preheat the air fryer to 184ºC. 2. In a large bowl, combine the plain flour, kosher salt, baking powder, ground cinnamon, light brown sugar, granulated sugar, canola oil, egg, vanilla extract, quick-cooking oats, and raisins. 3. Spray a baking pan with nonstick cooking spray, then pour the oat mixture into the pan and press down to evenly distribute. Place the pan in the air fryer and bake for 15 minutes or until golden brown. 4. Remove from the air fryer and allow to cool in the pan on a wire rack for 20 minutes before slicing and serving.

Pumpkin Pudding with Vanilla Wafers

Prep time: 10 minutes | Cook time: 12 to 17 minutes | Serves 4

250 g canned no-salt-added	1 tablespoon unsalted butter,
pumpkin purée (not pumpkin	melted
pie filling)	1 teaspoon pure vanilla extract
50 g packed brown sugar	4 low-fat vanilla, or plain
3 tablespoons plain flour	wafers, crumbled
1 egg, whisked	Nonstick cooking spray
2 tablespoons milk	

1. Preheat the air fryer to 176ºC. Coat a baking pan with nonstick cooking spray. Set aside. 2. Mix the pumpkin purée, brown sugar, flour, whisked egg, milk, melted butter, and vanilla in a medium bowl and whisk to combine. Transfer the mixture to the baking pan. 3. Place the baking pan in the air fryer basket and bake for 12 to 17 minutes until set. 4. Remove the pudding from the basket to a wire rack to cool. 5. Divide the pudding into four bowls and serve with the vanilla wafers sprinkled on top.

Coconut Macaroons

Prep time: 5 minutes | Cook time: 8 to 10 minutes | Makes 12 macaroons

120 g desiccated, sweetened coconut	2 tablespoons sugar
4½ teaspoons plain flour	1 egg white
	½ teaspoon almond extract

1. Preheat the air fryer to 164°C. 2. In a medium bowl, mix all ingredients together. 3. Shape coconut mixture into 12 balls. 4. Place all 12 macaroons in air fryer basket. They won't expand, so you can place them close together, but they shouldn't touch. 5. Air fry for 8 to 10 minutes, until golden.

Baked Apples and Walnuts

Prep time: 6 minutes | Cook time: 20 minutes | Serves 4

4 small Granny Smith apples	1 teaspoon ground cinnamon
50 g chopped walnuts	½ teaspoon ground nutmeg
50 g light brown sugar	120 ml water, or apple juice
2 tablespoons butter, melted	

1. Cut off the top third of the apples. Spoon out the core and some of the flesh and discard. Place the apples in a small air fryer baking pan. 2. Insert the crisper plate into the basket and the basket into the unit. Preheat to 176°C. 3. In a small bowl, stir together the walnuts, brown sugar, melted butter, cinnamon, and nutmeg. Spoon this mixture into the centers of the hollowed-out apples. 4. Once the unit is preheated, pour the water into the crisper plate. Place the baking pan into the basket. 5. Bake for 20 minutes. 6. When the cooking is complete, the apples should be bubbly and fork tender.

Baked Peaches with Yogurt and Blueberries

Prep time: 10 minutes | Cook time: 7 to 11 minutes | Serves 6

3 peaches, peeled, halved, and pitted	285 g plain Greek yogurt
2 tablespoons packed brown sugar	¼ teaspoon ground cinnamon
	1 teaspoon pure vanilla extract
	190 g fresh blueberries

1. Preheat the air fryer to 192°C. 2. Arrange the peaches in the air fryer basket, cut side up. Top with a generous sprinkle of brown sugar. 3. Bake in the preheated air fryer for 7 to 11 minutes, or until the peaches are lightly browned and caramelized. 4. Meanwhile, whisk together the yogurt, cinnamon, and vanilla in a small bowl until smooth. 5. Remove the peaches from the basket to a plate. Serve topped with the yogurt mixture and fresh blueberries.

Cinnamon and Pecan Pie

Prep time: 10 minutes | Cook time: 25 minutes | Serves 4

1 pack shortcrust pastry	⅛ teaspoon nutmeg
½ teaspoons cinnamon	3 tablespoons melted butter, divided
¾ teaspoon vanilla extract	2 tablespoons sugar
2 eggs	65 g chopped pecans
175 ml maple syrup	

1. Preheat the air fryer to 188°C. 2. In a small bowl, coat the pecans in 1 tablespoon of melted butter. 3. Transfer the pecans to the air fryer and air fry for about 10 minutes. 4. Put the pie dough in a greased pie pan, trim off the excess and add the pecans on top. 5. In a bowl, mix the rest of the ingredients. Pour this over the pecans. 6. Put the pan in the air fryer and bake for 25 minutes. 7. Serve immediately.

Pecan and Cherry Stuffed Apples

Prep time: 10 minutes | Cook time: 20 minutes | Serves 4

4 apples (about 565 g)	3 tablespoons brown sugar
40 g chopped pecans	¼ teaspoon allspice
50 g dried tart cherries	Pinch salt
1 tablespoon melted butter	Ice cream, for serving

1. Cut off top ½ inch from each apple; reserve tops. With a melon baller, core through stem ends without breaking through the bottom. (Do not trim bases.) 2. Preheat the air fryer to 176°C. Combine pecans, cherries, butter, brown sugar, allspice, and a pinch of salt. Stuff mixture into the hollow centers of the apples. Cover with apple tops. Put in the air fryer basket, using tongs. Air fry for 20 to 25 minutes, or just until tender. 3. Serve warm with ice cream.

Coconut-Custard Pie

Prep time: 10 minutes | Cook time: 20 to 23 minutes | Serves 4

240 ml milk	2 eggs
50 g granulated sugar, plus 2 tablespoons	2 tablespoons melted butter
30 g scone mix	Cooking spray
1 teaspoon vanilla extract	50 g desiccated, sweetened coconut

1. Place all ingredients except coconut in a medium bowl. 2. Using a hand mixer, beat on high speed for 3 minutes. 3. Let sit for 5 minutes. 4. Preheat the air fryer to 164°C. 5. Spray a baking pan with cooking spray and place pan in air fryer basket. 6. Pour filling into pan and sprinkle coconut over top. 7. Cook pie for 20 to 23 minutes or until center sets.

Boston Cream Donut Holes

Prep time: 30 minutes | Cook time: 4 minutes per batch | Makes 24 donut holes

200 g bread flour

1 teaspoon active dry yeast

1 tablespoon granulated sugar

¼ teaspoon salt

120 ml warm milk

½ teaspoon pure vanilla extract

2 egg yolks

2 tablespoons unsalted butter, melted

Vegetable oil

Custard Filling:

95 g box French vanilla instant pudding mix

175 ml whole milk

60 ml heavy cream

Chocolate Glaze:

170 g chocolate chips

80 ml heavy cream

1. Combine the flour, yeast, sugar, and salt in the bowl of a stand mixer. Add the milk, vanilla, egg yolks and butter. Mix until the dough starts to come together in a ball. Transfer the dough to a floured surface and knead the dough by hand for 2 minutes. Shape the dough into a ball, place it in a large, oiled bowl, cover the bowl with a clean kitchen towel and let the dough rise for 1 to 1½ hours or until the dough has doubled in size. 2. When the dough has risen, punch it down and roll it into a 24-inch log. Cut the dough into 24 pieces and roll each piece into a ball. Place the dough balls on a baking sheet and let them rise for another 30 minutes. 3. Preheat the air fryer to 204ºC. 4. Spray or brush the dough balls lightly with vegetable oil and air fry eight at a time for 4 minutes, turning them over halfway through the cooking time. 5. While donut holes are cooking, make the filling and chocolate glaze. Make the filling: Use an electric hand mixer to beat the French vanilla pudding, milk and ¼ cup of heavy cream together for 2 minutes. 6. Make the chocolate glaze: Place the chocolate chips in a medium-sized bowl. Bring the heavy cream to a boil on the stovetop and pour it over the chocolate chips. Stir until the chips are melted and the glaze is smooth. 7. To fill the donut holes, place the custard filling in a pastry bag with a long tip. Poke a hole into the side of the donut hole with a small knife. Wiggle the knife around to make room for the filling. Place the pastry bag tip into the hole and slowly squeeze the custard into the center of the donut. Dip the top half of the donut into the chocolate glaze, letting any excess glaze drip back into the bowl. Let the glazed donut holes sit for a few minutes before serving

Printed in Great Britain
by Amazon

21014888R00045